Towards Effort

The advanced guide

Towards Effortless Activity
The advanced guide to enlightenment

by

The Implicate Technology Centre

The Implicate Technology Centre
London

First published in the United Kingdom in 1988 by
  The Implicate Technology Centre
  BCM ACT
  London WC1N 3XX

British Library Cataloguing in Publication Data

Implicate Technology Centre

Towards effortless activity: the
advanced guide to enlightenment.
1. Buddha and Buddhism 2. Mysticism
I. Title
294.3'442   BQ5660

ISBN 0-9511839-1-5

Typeset, printed and bound in the United Kingdom by
A. Wheaton & Co. Ltd, Exeter.

Beyond the personality: the beginner's guide to enlightenment and *Towards effortless activity: the advanced guide to enlightenment* are published by The Implicate Technology Centre Limited.

The Implicate Technology Centre has been formed to meet the extensive need for self-help books of a primarily secular nature, which explain in clear, direct and everyday terms what enlightenment is and how it can be attained.

Contents

Preface

This is the second of two books which together provide a systematic and coherent system of meditation leading to the final stage of enlightenment. This book completes the direct and practical Western meditative system begun in *Beyond the personality: the beginner's guide to enlightenment*. Together, these two books teach ordinary people how to become enlightened without surrendering the intellect or renouncing everyday life.

In the West, we have available to us an abundance of spiritual teachings. Virtually none of those teachings contains effective and practical instruction on how to attain enlightenment, or unity with God. You can dedicate many years to the study and practice of such teachings, gaining much by way of intellectual knowledge and little by way of direct experience of the truths sought.

If you have invested your time, your energy and even your money in pursuing spiritual experience along those other paths, you may feel that you are qualified to start with the advanced meditative practices taught in this book. This is unlikely to produce satisfactory results. If you have genuinely made spiritual progress through another teaching, then you should be able to make very rapid progress through the basic meditation taught in *Beyond the personality: the beginner's guide to enlightenment*.

The Implicate Technology Centre

I *Introduction to the Implicate Technology model of reality*

There is only one reality. Reality is one. This secular teaching, and all religions, can be understood as models of the one reality, relevant to particular cultures over particular time periods.

Who should read this book?

Just as no one can eat your food for you, so no one can give you enlightenment. Only you can take yourself to the ultimate goal of realising the final stage of enlightenment. This book will provide you with practical advice and guidance on how to attain this unparalled state of freedom. The determination and commitment to succeed must stem from you alone.

Any intelligent person can read this book, particularly this intro-ductory chapter, and, after reflecting on its contents, be able to develop an intellectual understanding of the nature of reality and the experience of enlightenment. This will convey as much about reality and the experience of enlightenment as a chemical analysis of food content and nutritional value will convey about the experience of eating a tasty, well-cooked meal. Intellectual appreciation is no substitute for the understanding gained through experience.

In this secular Implicate Technology teaching, the first stage of actual spiritual understanding based on experience is called the psychological enlightenment. That state of mind, and the corresponding freedom from emotional and intellectual ties, is attainable by any ordinary, intelligent person willing to give one hundred days of committed daily practice to meditation, for a minimum of fifteen minutes daily. This book's precursor, *Beyond the personality: the beginner's guide to enlightenment* teaches you how to attain the psychological stage of enlightenment, which is a

1

necessary prerequisite to the advanced meditations taught in this book.

Many who have attained this first stage of psychological enlightenment may find themselves resting at that point on the far journey to realisation of the final stage of enlightenment. There is no harm in that, provided that one who does so both continues with daily practice of meditation and uses the teachings in this book to understand the journey that lies ahead. Careful reflection on these teachings will help you to realise both what you have achieved and how far you have yet to travel.

This book is written to assist those who have reached the first stage of enlightened understanding, i.e., psychological enlightenment, as taught in *The beginner's guide to enlightenment*, and who are committed to further progress along the path. The commitment is to yourself, and yet this Implicate Technology path will also teach you meditative skills which will enhance your inherent ability to heal and transform the lives of others. One who successfully follows this path will become empowered, through the natural process of self-development, to act as a healing agent in the development and transformation of our culture.

Those committed to proceeding along this secular path to the realisation of the final stage of enlightenment should place their faith and their trust in these teachings – a faith balanced equally with faith in their own ability fully to realise enlightenment. Accept and follow the advice in this book without making the error of thinking that the individual is, or should be, free to pick and choose as a matter of course. Where choice is given in these teachings, choose freely and wisely; where choice is limited, learn to accept the limitations as being necessary to direct you towards the absolute and priceless goal – the limitless freedom of the final stage of enlightenment.

The goal is reached through developing a genuine, unselfish and unselfseeking humility. As you progress along the path, you will come to understand that your sense of individuality is part of the illusion. Be clear: it is not you who lives, but that which lives you.

Ordinary life, as experienced and understood by the unenlightened mind, is a product of ignorance and illusion. Ordinary life, as experienced and understood by the enlightened mind, is clarity, wisdom and delight. The movement, stage by stage, from ignorance to enlightenment is achieved through realising the illusory nature of the ego, the individual sense of 'I'.

This secular Implicate Technology teaching will enable you to make that transition from ignorance to enlightenment by providing detailed and practical instruction on:

1. A fully articulated model of reality, which describes how reality works and explains your central role in the process that is reality;

2. Setting yourself clearly on the path to realising unity: the transition to an intermediate state of enlightened understanding, begun in chapter 5 of *The beginner's guide to enlightenment*, is set in a wider cultural and personal context;

3. The second stage of enlightenment, the attainment of a still mind: a mind capable of concentrating on one thought at a time, for as long as is necessary;

4. The third stage of enlightenment, the awakening of the transcendental mind: a mind capable of glimpsing dimly and briefly at first, and then, as understanding develops, capable of experiencing clearly and for sustained periods the underlying transcendental nature of what seems objectively real to the five senses;

5. The fourth and final stage of enlightenment, the development of a mind integrated and unified with all of reality: a mind which sees only the inherent unity of all that is, and that all separateness of people, places and things is illusory;

6. The four formless absorptions: explorations of the final stage of enlightenment, designed to round out and enhance the newly enlightened mind.

All of this will be taught with the help of simple and practical meditative disciplines which use the ordinary experiences of everyday life as their raw material.

What follows in this chapter is written from a perspective rooted in the realisation of the final stage of enlightenment. This material makes no concessions to the limitations of unenlightened minds. It is written for the guidance and benefit of those who seek the final stage of enlightenment.

Return to this chapter again and again as you travel along the path. Your understanding will change and deepen as you make progress with the advanced meditations in this book. As your understanding moves from the merely intellectual to the intuitive certainty of direct under-

3

standing based on experience, you will be able to measure your progress towards realising the final stage of enlightenment.

☆　　☆　　☆　　☆

What is the nature of the final stage of enlightenment?

To answer this question it is necessary to develop two reference points, seemingly poles apart and yet in reality an eternal and transcendent unity. To comply with Implicate Technology disciplines, the words used must be part of ordinary life. To function in a fully developed, clearly articulated model of reality, the words must direct your awareness to the two primary aspects of reality whose interaction creates all which we experience.

This refers to the totality of conditioned existence, infinitely varied through time, infinitely extended through space[1]. Every thought, every action, every person, every thing, animate or inanimate, is embraced in this. There is no aspect of your life which is not part of this, shaped and influenced by the constantly changing interactions of the ten conditions.

That refers to the natural state of the unconditioned mind. That is devoid of conditioned qualities, devoid of shape or form or feature. None of the ten conditions, which limit and constrain our lives, apply to that.

Practice of the meditation techniques taught in this book will show you, through your own experience, that this and that are an indistinguishable unity. This is simply that subject to the ten conditions. This is the content, the materialised and conditioned thought process of that, the unconditioned and all-embracing universal mind.

Conditioned existence, this, and unconditioned awareness, that, form a perfect and eternal unity – a continuous and unbroken act of transcendental delight. This and that are joined in an eternal, blissful act of union – in the words of other models of reality: God and the world are ever one, Siva and Sakti are ever engaged in sexual union, and Samsara and Nirvana are ever two aspects of the one, inexpressible unity. From the unenlightened point of view, this can only, because of ignorance of the real nature of that, be experienced illusorily, as life's transient joys and sorrows, pains and pleasures.

Of necessity, all fully developed models of the one reality have certain features in common. Hinduism uses Brahman to represent the im-

---

[1]   See *The beginner's guide to enlightenment*, chapter 3.

4

manent transcendental reality, Buddhism uses the Void and Implicate Technology uses that. Similarly, each model presents a practical path to perceiving the threefold nature of transcendental reality.

Hinduism presents a path to realising Brahman as Sat-Chit-Ananda, as Being-Conciousness-Bliss. Buddhism presents a path to realising the Void as three dualities comprising a unity: Bliss and the Void, the Clear Light and the Void, Wisdom and the Void. This teaching of Implicate Technology presents a path to realising the nature of that as untainted *clarity* in perceiving what is, *wisdom* to accept what is, and *delight* in what is.

Images of reality used within the context of a fully developed model of reality will control, direct and focus your ever-growing awareness – these images will help you to make sense of this as you struggle to realise that within yourself. These root images form the basis of the Implicate Technology model of reality. These images are simply a form of words to direct your attention to the true nature of what you experience, and simultaneously to help you understand the nature of the fully enlightened mind.

The true nature of reality, this and that in eternal union, is conciousness without content, which nonetheless permits all contents to exist. The direct experience of that, as experienced every day by the enlightened mind, is a formless, still and silent experience, impossible to convey in words and knowable only by direct experience. The direct experience of this, as experienced every day by the enlightened mind, is an unfailing acceptance of what is, devoid of judgement, inhibition or interference.

Your everyday experience of this, of yourself and others as apparently separate and different from each other and all else, is an illusion of the unenlightenend mind. Committed practice of the meditation techniques taught in this book will progressively cleanse your mind of its illusory sense of separateness. The experience of enlightenment is like awakening from a dream – the illusion is broken and your true nature, the true nature of all reality, becomes clear and transcends all configurations of the ten conditions.

The underlying nature of everything perceptible to your senses, this, is a formless immanent conciousness devoid of qualities, that. These Implicate Technology meditative disciplines, practised as taught, without arrogant picking and choosing according to individual wish, will gradually free your mind from the conditions constraining its original and true nature. When you have overcome the self-limiting tendencies of your mind, this will be revealed as that.

5

This is not the creation of that. There is no such duality as 'perceptible reality' and 'the creator of that reality'. To the enlightened mind, this is that.

That is not separate from this. That is simultaneously the source, the substance and the real nature of this. Put simply, you are that: the enlightened mind is aware of this ultimate nature of perceptible reality as direct intuitive experience; the unenlightened mind is not – such awareness is the only real difference between the two.

How is the world experienced after enlightenment?

Before a person sets out on the long inward journey to enlightenment, the world is experienced as quite ordinary. People are understood and accepted as people, places as places and things as things. Life is constrained and conditioned by your attitude to your needs and desires, duties and responsibilities.

Once you enter, knowingly or unknowingly, on the eventful path to enlightenment, all of your apparently ordinary experience changes. You develop a tendency to interpret your life in terms of richly significant hidden meanings. Everything – people, places, events, things – becomes liable to be understood by you as, in reality, something mystical and meaningful.

Prior to realising the final and absolute stage of enlightenment, you have a tendency to distinguish between ordinary people and those extraordinary people who seem to possess and understand secret knowledge. You may feel yourself to be developing sage-like qualities; or you may find yourself seeking out someone who seems to you to have such qualities. In any event, the world will frequently seem to you an extraordinary place, full of mysterious and hidden potential.

The purpose of enlightenment is to realise, through experience, final and absolute understanding of the indivisible and unified nature of perceptible reality. This is the end result of a process entirely different in nature from the mere acquisition of intellectual knowledge. Once a person has realised the final state of enlightenment, the world is again experienced as quite ordinary.

Before setting out on the path to enlightenment, this is understood as being ordinary. While on the path, this is understood to be richly significant and filled with mysterious potential. When the goal has been realised, this is understood again as being ordinary.

For one who has realised the goal of conditioned existence, this is understood through direct experience as that. Such is the everyday experience of any enlightened person. Through clarity, wisdom and delight, everything is experienced just as it is, understood and experienced simultaneously in its manifest and unmanifest forms.

The experience of enlightenment is like waking up from a dream. What was once perceived as real is now understood to have only relative reality. In the final analysis of the enlightened mind, what once preoccupied consiousness is now understood through direct experience to be thoroughly illusory.

Included in the contents of the dream, the great web of illusion which constitutes conditioned existence, are all the everyday concerns – hopes, fears, desires, ambitions and values – which comprise the individual sense of 'I'. The awakening comes when this is experienced within the clear, tranquil, impersonal and absolute subjectivity of the unconditioned mind. The unenlightened mind, operating illusorily through the individual sense of 'I', sees this as separate and divisible, as people, places and things; the enlightened mind, operating clearly through the absence of the illusory sense of the individual 'I', sees this as people, places and things, and simultaneously sees this as that, and only as that, one and indivisible.

The unenlightened person's experience of reality, being relative, is obscured by a fog of thoughts, emotions, needs and desires. These inner activities are the product of the relatively real individual mind; practice of the meditation techniques taught in this book will awaken you to a true and lasting understanding of the relatively illusory nature of the individual mind. The enlightened person's experience of reality is clear and still, like a vast and motionless ocean. In the final silence of the absolute and all-embracing mind, fully conscious and devoid of all thought, reality is experienced directly as it is.

After the final stage of enlightenment, this is no longer understood or experienced as being comprised of separate elements. All of this is understood, by direct intuitive experience, to be the outward form and patterning of the all-embracing and unmanifest source, that. There is no longer a distinction to be understood between 'self' and 'others'.

After the final stage of enlightenment, you continue to live in ordinary, mundane ways. The body must be fed, cared for and rested. If necessary, a source of income has to be found to maintain oneself and any dependants.

After the final stage of enlightenment, the world is just the same, and yet completely different. Being no longer compulsively pre-occupied with motives, values, needs and desires, you act as an intuitive expression of the inherent implicate laws. You no longer act from a personal source or motive.

The enlightened person perceives both individuality and separateness, recognising them as illusory products of unenlightened experience, and simultaneously experiences everything as the material manifestation of a unified, all-embracing, immanent source. Choice of action is both meaningless and effortless after enlightenment. The enlightened person, clearly set face to face with reality, has no inner experience of individual choice or action.

With the dissolution of the individual sense of 'I' comes the realisation of the illusory nature of personal desires. The enlightened person is not exempt from the influence of karma; it is more accurate to say that the enlightened person simply does not act in such a way as to incur either negative or positive karmic consequences. The person who has realised through experience the final stage of enlightenment floats in an endless sea of karmic neutrality, freed of choices rooted in the illusory, personal sense of 'I'.

For the enlightened person, the formerly objective world vanishes. The world is no longer experienced within the context of a merely illusory objectivity; instead, the world is understood in its true nature, as an experience occurring through and within the final and absolute subjectivity of mind in its unconditioned state.

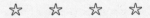

If I am <u>that</u>, if my true nature is immanent all-embracing transcendent being, how can I learn to experience this?

In common with Eastern implicate technologies such as Taoism, Buddhism and Hinduism, this Implicate Technology meditative system directs the awareness of the meditator to address one central issue during advanced meditative practices: who is it who is doing the meditation? The answer obtained from carefully following each meditative system to its natural conclusion is always the same: when sought in a rigorous and disciplined manner, the meditator simply cannot be found. This result is, of course, not at all apparent to ordinary common sense.

8

Advanced meditation teaches the meditator that the sense of 'I', the inherent sense of being an individual and separate person, has only relative reality. It has no absolute foundation in reality. At all times and in all circumstances, the sense of specific and unique individuality is a relative illusion, created by the interactions of the ten conditions.

From the unenlightened point of view, the sense of 'I', the natural and spontaneous feeling of specific individuality, is part of everyday life and taken for granted. From the enlightened point of view, the sense of 'I' is understood, through direct intuitive experience, to have no more validity as a focus for experience of this than the emotional pains and joys of life are found to have after the attainment of the psychological stage of enlightenment. When the relatively illusory sense of 'I', the individual ego, fades away, the true nature of reality is understood.

'The "I" casts off the illusion of "I" and yet remains as "I". Such is the paradox of Self-Realisation. The realised do not see any contradiction in it.'[1]

With the fading of the illusory sense of individual separateness, the enlightened mind sees all as a manifestation of that. 'I', 'you', these words and the thought running through your mind at this instant, are all manifestations of that. As the thought process of the one, universal mind unfolds, so this unfolds through time and space: simultaneously that is realised as stillness, emptiness and as being devoid of qualities, and experienced as clarity, wisdom and delight.

A central image in the Implicate Technology model of reality is: reality is a process whose function is to guide you towards enlightenment, at a pace and in circumstances suitable to your own nature. The process can be understood as the workings of an infinite organic machine, a unified and coherent whole in which each component part is meaningfully located. You are the focus of the process; you are a key element in the machine.

The beginner's guide to enlightenment teaches that all the material you need to assist you in your journey along the path to enlightenment is to be found in your own life. Karma shapes your life to guide and direct you, through the process that is reality. Throw yourself with commitment and dedication into these Implicate Technology teachings and you will realise the final stage of enlightenment through direct intuitive experience.

---

[1] *Talks with Sri Ramana Maharshi*; Sri Ramanasramam, Tiruvannamalai, T. N. Venkataraman, 1984; page 29.

Meditation, the primary tool available to you to help you to realise the enlightened state of mind, needs nothing outside of yourself and only the simplest of conditions: this is because reality is a coherent and integrated process, an entirely organic and unified machine. The goal of meditation is reached when the thought process can be switched off at will, leaving a consciousness clear about what is, wise in accepting what is and filled with delight at <u>that</u>. This state of mind, which involves gaining control over the very source of your own thought process through undistracted alertness, is known in Eastern implicate technology systems as samadhi.

Samadhi is a state of mind sustained over longer and longer periods until it becomes permanent, which begins spontaneously with the most strenuous and intense period of concentration possible. As your samadhi develops, you learn to analyse the processes of your mind, gradually discovering the true nature of mental processes. The conclusion of the process of samadhi is the realisation of an eternal state of mind which is serenely aware of what is and is unsullied by the thought process.

The great literature of all religions is filled with descriptions of the state of mind which is the goal of this secular teaching. To realise <u>this</u> as <u>that</u> is to see the world as Brahman, to become at one with God, to realise the Void, to reunite with the Tao. The differences between these forms of expression are simply cultural variations of the one inexpressible truth of reality, which is knowable only through direct intuitive experience.

How can you measure your progress along the path leading to the final stage of enlightenment?

The natural tendency of the unenlightened mind is to seek proof or confirmation of the teaching. Where a person's mind is relatively underdeveloped, there will be a correspondingly strong desire to seek objective proof. Not only will such an attitude probably fail to lead to the desired evidence, but it will also fail to lead to enlightenment.

The reason for this is straightforward. In common with all other fully-developed models of reality, Implicate Technology teaches that the true nature of reality can only be understood through realising by direct experience the absolute, final and all-embracing subjectivity which informs and comprises perceptible reality. A dependence on mere

10

objectivity is an essential part of the illusion preventing you from knowing directly that conditioned existence is an organic and integrated unity.

If you are to transcend the illusion binding you to non-enlightened states of mind, you must transcend your mind's mistaken tendency to regard the world as being comprised of objective phenomena. Equally, do not make the mistake of thinking that the world somehow exists only in your imagination. Remember always, reality is this: that people and places, things and events, the individual sense of 'I', and even the thought passing through your mind as you read this – all of this – is the thought process of the all-embracing, unconditioned, unqualified, universal and only mind, made manifest in conditioned form.

All the contents of a dream – people, places, things and events – are known on waking to be the product of the dreaming mind. What was experienced as real during the dream is known, on waking, to be merely a product of the dreaming mind. Similarly, when the absolute and impersonal subjectivity of mind in its unconditioned state is realised, then this is truly understood in its illusory nature, like awakening from a dream.

To seek proof in a form objectively demonstrable to others is to miss the point of enlightenment. If you are to realise the freedom of the final stage of enlightenment, you must learn to lessen your dependence on merely objective ways of understanding reality. Any proof must be of a kind to cause you to develop reliance on impersonal and autonomous subjective processes if it is to lead you towards understanding the true nature of conditioned existence.

This section introduces two examples of autonomous and impersonal subjective processes. Their occurrence on the path to enlightenment is common, and, at first, dramatic and exciting. In the end, as your mind progresses in understanding through experience, you will realise the transitory and illusory nature of these experiences and leave them far behind.

Not everyone will have these specific experiences. The final stage of enlightenment can be attained without, for example, any recollection of previous lives. You will spontaneously have those experiences which are relevant to the needs of your own developing nature.

All your experiences are a function of the activity of karma: their purpose, appropriate to your needs to develop in understanding, is to direct you towards a true and clear experience of reality. Resist the temptation to be beguiled by such experiences: to become dependent on

11

their appearing or not appearing is to seek out fool's gold. Learn what these experiences have to teach you, then leave them behind.

The first commonly experienced subjective process – remembrance of past lives – is a natural by-product of the advanced meditative techniques taught in this book. This current life is simply one of many incarnations you have experienced. You can prove this, to yourself, by developing the capacity for intuitive recollection of previous lives through advanced meditation.

The process of reincarnation is a natural product of the inherent implicate law of karma. A mind which has not yet realised the absolute and final subjectivity of reality is inexorably and endlessly bound to the process of death and rebirth. Again and again and again, as many times as each consciousness individually requires, the inexorable process of reality creates fresh opportunities, through the life experience of each incarnation, for the individual mind to progress along the path of recognising the illusory nature of mere objectivity.

All that you have experienced, in this and previous lives, remains in your memory. Your intuition, enhanced by the meditative practices taught in this book, can enable you to recollect your past lives. According to what is released into consciousness from your memory, so you can monitor your progress towards enlightenment.

The more details you can recall from a previous life, the further you are from enlightenment. Just as a complete recall of the details of this current life would be of little help in understanding the karmic significance of the events of this life, so, too, an obsession with detailed memories of past lives would be of little help in identifying the necessary actions to take you to enlightenment. A mind which carries an accumulation of facts and figures, chronologies and histories, both individual and general, is a mind ill-equipped to realise the final stage of enlightenment.

The key to measuring progress towards the realisation of that is the extent to which your recall of past lives is based on understanding their significance and meaning in terms of an accumulation of experience. When you grasp your previous lives as a progression of understanding, then you will be better able to identify the karmic direction of this life. A mind which is capable of identifying patterns of meaning from latent impressions deep in memory is a mind well-equipped to realise the unconditioned state.

Do not set out energetically and with determination to recall the traces of past lives. If such confirmatory experiences are to come your

12

way, they will happen spontaneously. Simply listen carefully to the promptings of your intuition.

An association with a place, person or object, or an event witnessed or read about, may stimulate latent traces of past lives to rise to consciousness. The experience is one of recognising or remembering something familiar and long forgotten. Although at first such an experience may seem extraordinary, it is no more remarkable than the common occurrence of remembering a long forgotten incident.

It is very unlikely that you will find any objective confirmation of these traces in your memory. The benefit of the experience is realised by accepting the evidence of your intuition. Only you can decide if such experiences are valid for you. If you accept them on their own terms, you progress along the path through recognising and accepting such experiences as real.

The second subjective process, commonly experienced as you progress towards the purifying and clarifying state of samadhi, is the phenomenon of visions. These are seen by the inner eye and heard by the inner ear, in a manner of speaking. The experience is startlingly realistic: it is as if, instead of watching a film as an observer, you were to suddenly find yourself in the midst of the events portrayed.

Visions are not mere imaginings of the mind: they are experienced spontaneously and autonomously. Visions can relate to past, present or future; their material can be of a personal or a general nature, encompassing any aspect of reality. Visions are a genuine reflection of significantly related aspects of reality, in, and for the benefit of, an individual consciousness.

As with memories of earlier incarnations, you are unlikely to find any objective confirmation of a vision. You should resist the temptation to rely on visions as prophecies of the future: a mind developing towards the clarity of the final stage of enlightenment must learn to live in and for the here and now, never in or for the past or the future. Visions are best understood as an internal, autonomous form of self-tuition.

Visions function as a means of drawing to the attention of a developing consciousness aspects of reality which, from the point of view of that consciousness, are significantly related. Typically, the central message you are being taught is refined through an iterative series of partially repeated, constantly developing visions. The important point is to transcend the detail of the vision, and grasp intuitively what it is trying to teach you about yourself.

At first the experience of visions, like recollecting the latent traces of

13

past lives held in memory, is exhilarating, breathtaking and wonderful, or perhaps fearful and terrible. In time, as the practice of meditation advances and the individual consciousness becomes aware of the relatively illusory nature of individuality, the importance and relevance of all such phenomena will fade away. They are in the end no more than educational experiences along the way.

2   *The path to samadhi*

There are ten conditions, not nine, ten conditions, not eleven. Every situation which you experience consists of a particular configuration of the ten conditions – karma; space and time; physical, emotional and intellectual limiting factors; moral and social constraints, and political and economic pressures. The goal of Implicate Technology, as of all fully developed models of reality, is to guide you to realisation through direct experience of the pure and original state of mind transcending all conditions.

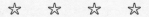

How can an ordinary person, inevitably subject to birth, ageing, suffering and death, transform and transcend the conditions which bind and limit every life?

Know this as a certainty, provable only by direct experience: there is a state of mind not subject to birth, ageing, suffering and death. That state of mind is the source from which springs all of <u>this</u>, the complete cycle of conditioned existence. Your destiny, sooner or later, in this life or some other, is to re-unite with the original, all-embracing, unconditioned state of being, <u>that</u>.

The nature of reality is such that you are free to choose whether or not to embark on a spiritual path. Be clear: if you choose, for any reason at all, not to work at your spiritual self-development, you incur an invariable compensating response from the unified process that is reality. That is to say, if you ignore your spiritual self-progress, the inevitable consequence is birth, ageing, suffering and death – repeated endlessly.

These four – birth, ageing, suffering and death – are the unvarying experience of each one of your lives. Everything else – all joys, happinesses, achievements, loves and possessions – is transient and subject to change and loss. The only escape from this endlessly repetitive cycle of

15

conditioned existence is the triumphant freedom gained by attaining enlightenment.

To achieve the unparalleled and unlimited freedom from all burdens which is the natural experience of mind in its fully enlightened state, you must learn how to rid your mind gradually of the ignorance of its own nature accumulated throughout your previous incarnations. Chapters 3 to 6 of this book teach you, step by step, how to shed the layers of ignorance obscuring direct experience of the mind in its natural state. This process of shaking off ignorance of the true nature of reality and of abiding, at first with great effort but eventually effortlessly, in direct experience of that, is known in most Eastern implicate technology systems as samadhi.

Samadhi begins spontaneously with the most intense period of concentration you will have encountered to date. Chapters 3 to 6 of this book will guide you from that raw and unstructured first experience of samadhi through a detailed set of yoga exercises which will awaken you to the true nature of your mind. At the end of your practice of these exercises, provided that you work within the guidelines given, you will realise the full, final and absolute stage of enlightenment. Regardless of the conditions of your life, your experience will be of limitless freedom and effortless activity.

This chapter teaches you how to live your life in such a way that samadhi begins spontaneously. You cannot force the beginning of samadhi. Samadhi will only occur spontaneously *and* in a mind which has been prepared for the experience through a life lived in harmony with the moral purpose inherent in karma.

If it is your natural inclination to work within a religious model of reality, rather than this secular Implicate Technology model, you can readily adapt these exercises to devotional purposes. The practice of the exercises remains the same for religious or secular purposes. The goal, if you are religious by nature, is not realisation of the Godhead – mind in its unconditioned state – rather, to the religiously inclined person, the goal is achieved through realising one's inherent unity with God. In Implicate Technology terms, this is the realisation that all of this is one and inseparable.

The distinction between realising the unconditioned state and dwelling in the love of God is simply one of individual preference and perspective. Chapter 5, *The path to the final stage of enlightenment*, teaches where the meditations end if your goal is full realisation of your devotion to God. Appendix 1, *How to recognise a fully developed model of reality*, clarifies the differences between the devotional path to understanding reality and the path to knowledge of reality.

All the conditions of life—including birth, ageing, suffering and death—can be transcended through the practice of samadhi, the clear setting face to face with reality. The capacity to experience samadhi, and so to be able to rise above and transform the conditions of life, is only given to a person who is in harmony with the evolutionary purpose of karma. This chapter teaches you how to live an ordinary life, in the midst of conditions, which takes you towards the priceless gift of samadhi—a still, clear mind perceiving <u>this</u> in its true nature as <u>that</u>.

What is the moral purpose inherent in karma?

Mind in its pure original unconditioned state, <u>that</u>, makes manifest its inherent unity and harmony through karma. The workings of karma form, shape and establish the coherent, inter-related and meaningful contexts in which every aspect and activity of your life takes place. Karma works at every moment to direct you along the path towards a full, final and absolute understanding of your own nature, <u>that</u>.

As you will come to realise through practice of the advanced meditative techniques taught in this book, <u>this</u> is simply the externalised and materialised thought process of <u>that</u>, the all-embracing unconditioned mind which transcends and embraces conditioned existence. Your own thoughts spring from, and return to, <u>that</u>. Your own thoughts and actions are woven together inextricably with karma, as <u>this</u> unfolds spontaneously, now, in the clear sight of <u>that</u>.

It is crucial to understand the link between your own thought process and karma. <u>This</u> can be understood as a process designed to purge you of your ignorance that <u>this</u> is <u>that</u>. Karma is the implicate law, inherent in <u>this</u>, which reacts to your thoughts and actions so as to guide you towards realisation of <u>that</u>.

The moral purpose inherent in karma is to teach you that all things are interconnected. The apparent separateness of people, places, events and things is an illusion experienced and suffered by mind in its unenlightened form. The true nature of <u>this</u> is an organic unity, a vast, evolving, inherently harmonious thought process, in which each part is dependent on all the others.

Just as you are a central part of <u>this</u>, so, in the same way, each person

17

and all else is inseparable from the whole. A thought or an action which results in harm ocurring to another part of this, acts against the harmony inherent in the process by which this unfolds through time and space. The extent and severity of the karmic compensating response depends on how much the harmonious flow of reality has been disturbed, and on the specific needs of the consciousnesses involved.

This Implicate Technology teaching on the moral purpose inherent in karma is simply a technical way of discussing the moral basis of a life lived in harmony. It is purely a matter of personal taste whether you prefer to live by this technical formulation of the compensating and educational nature of karma, or to work within a religious code of ethics, such as the teachings of Christianity, Judaism, Islam, Hinduism or Buddhism. What counts is what you learn from your life's experiences and the choices which you make concerning others, through your thought and action.

You cannot escape the consequences of your thoughts and actions. If you selfishly use or harm another part of this, you inevitably incur an appropriate and negative karmic response. If you unselfishly benefit another part of this, you inevitably incur an appropriate and positive karmic response.

Be clear: it is futile to anticipate the form of a karmic response to a particular action, either your own or another person's. Karma does not function to suit smug moral views or desires for revenge. Indeed, any attempt to second-guess karma will of itself incur an appropriate form of karmic compensation. The morally complacent, frequently sure of their good standing in God's eyes and filled with the illusory but deeply held conviction that they know God's purpose, are invariably taught a lesson in humility by karma.

All moral codes merely provide guidelines for behaviour. Adherence to a culturally approved moral code may get you the recognition and approval of others, but, unless your thoughts and actions genuinely reflect the harmony inherent in this, you will continue to suffer the karmic consequences of your lack of understanding. Fixed adherence to a moral code is no substitute for spontaneous and harmonious responses to the complexities and demands of late-twentieth century life.

The key to the Implicate Technology moral teaching is Act, as discussed in *The beginner's guide to enlightenment*. Act is a concise set of meditation-enhanced behavioural guidelines. Be guided by Act, and you will always react to situations in a spontaneous and harmonious manner.

18

The moral patterning inherent in the structure of reality is inescapable. From the religious point of view, karma is correctly understood as the expression of the will of God. From the secular Implicate Technology point of view, karma is correctly understood as the impersonal, implacable law ensuring that every thought and action incurs a compensating and balancing reaction.

You will enjoy or suffer the fruits of your thoughts and actions, whether it be in this life, in the after-death state or in any of your lives to come. Death will bring you no escape from the problems and difficulties of this life. Death simply provides you with a different set of opportunities to understand the true nature of this, a new set of conditions structured to lead you from ignorance to enlightenment.

From a devotional point of view, the primary cause of a person receiving the gift of samadhi is a life lived in accord with God's loving will. From the viewpoint of Implicate Technology, based not on the path of devotion to God but on the path of knowledge of reality, you will gain freedom from the constraints of this when you learn to behave with due regard to the inherent harmony and unity of this. Such a life, whether lived in a religious or a secular way, is lived according to the moral purpose inherent in the law of karma.

☆　　☆　　☆　　☆

How do you gain freedom from the constraints of conditioned existence, this?

The teachings in this chapter follow on from chapter 5 of *The beginner's guide to enlightenment*. That is to say, you are equipped to work with this chapter if you have realised the first or psychological stage of enlightenment. But you will not be equipped to deal with this chapter unless you have made a start on the transpersonal meditations in chapter 5 of that book.

In *The beginner's guide to enlightenment*, you were taught, step by practical step, how to develop your understanding through experience. As you developed in your practice of the meditation, your experience unfolded. Your experience was always used as the basis to draw you further along the path.

In this chapter, an apparently different approach will be used. First, you will be taught what may seem to be an entirely theoretical structure.

Then you will be taught how to prepare yourself to realise the theory in practice.

This technique is essentially the same as in the preparatory teachings. Before you can have the necessary experiences, you must develop your understanding. The understanding provided by meditating on the meaning of this chapter will prepare your mind for the expansions of consciousness to come.

The aim or goal of this chapter is to guide you towards a way of living which operates in harmony with the inherent implicate laws governing and informing our lives. This way of living does not impose any moral structure or expected pattern of behaviour on you. It is simply a way of living in harmony with the moral purpose inherent in reality.

The premise on which you will be taught to base your way of life is this: **your sense of being separate and an individual is entirely an illusion**. Naturally, this premise accords neither with common sense, legal structures or your own personal experience. Nonetheless the premise is true, as you will gradually come to understand through your own experience.

Through practice of the meditations taught in this book you will come to understand the relative, and therefore illusory, nature of what seems to be individual and separate experience. These teachings form a graded series of practical exercises which will develop and strengthen your awareness and understanding of the processes of your mind. You will come to understand through experience that all of reality, no matter how tangible and apparently separate from yourself, is a product of the mental processes of the one, unified, all-embracing mind.

Firstly, in chapter 2, you will learn a way of adapting, a way of living, which sets you in harmony with the flow of reality. It is essential that you learn to understand, accept and act in accord with the flow of reality. A mind pre-occupied with its own needs and desires is incapable of receiving the gift of samadhi.

Secondly, in chapter 3, you will learn the preliminary mental exercises which will accustom you to working with the thought process itself. Your experience of samadhi will be refined and purified, until you experience the stillness and serenity at the core of your mind. Simultaneously with experiencing the mind's natural stillness, you will develop a one-pointed mind, a mind fit to explore the true nature of reality.

Thirdly, in chapter 4, you will develop direct intuitive experience of the transcendental nature of this. You will meditate intensively on one thought at a time, for as long as you need to, until your mind develops understanding. You will experience an unshakeable shift in understanding—from experiencing everyday life as <u>this</u> to experiencing everyday life as <u>that</u>.

Fourthly, in chapter 5, you will experience through simple meditations, accessible only to the most developed of minds, the true, final and absolute nature of reality. You will come to understand that all apparently separate things are in reality one and undivided. You will also come to experience that all things unfold as the endless perfection and harmony of <u>that</u>.

Fifthly, in chapter 6, you will learn to explore reality from the basis of mind in its enlightened state. You will learn to explore <u>this</u> from a viewpoint which embraces and transcends space, time and karma. You will learn that you are an ordinary person, no different from anyone else; and the struggle to overcome your ignorance will be over.

How do you live your life in such a way that you receive the priceless gift of samadhi?

Reality is a process structured to purge you of your ignorance, accumulated through time, of the nature of <u>this</u>. Reality is a process structured to purge you of your ignorance, accumulated through time, of the nature of <u>that</u>. You can only understand that <u>this</u> is <u>that</u> through the experience of samadhi.

Samadhi only occurs in a mind adequately prepared for the experience. This Implicate Technology teaching of the clear setting face to face with reality prepares you in a twofold manner. Firstly, by teaching you how to live a life in harmony with the moral purpose of reality, and secondly, by teaching you yogic techniques which you can use in your everyday environment.

To live a life in harmony with the flow of reality you need a context which adequately describes and supports life as you live it. Other implicate technology[1] systems normally provide this through a culturally accepted moral code. This Implicate Technology teaching provides the context you need in terms of a description of the role of the individual in the process that is reality.

---

[1] See glossary for the distinction between implicate technology and Implicate Technology.

Our Western cultures place great importance on the rights and needs of the individual. Our governments talk freely of these rights but the reality varies according to the political needs and pressures of the moment. As taught in *The beginner's guide to enlightenment*, each one of us learns to deal with the world through the limits of our personality, insofar as the prevailing conditions will allow.

It is in accordance with the flow of reality, the nature of <u>this</u>, that the individual is treated as having such importance. Each one of us is a unique and essential source of experiencing <u>this</u> as it unfolds through time. To treat others with consideration for their needs and respect for their rights is to act in such a way as to incur positive karmic consequences; failure to help someone when it is within your gift, or to push aside the rights of another, invariably incurs negative karmic consequences.

It is in accordance with the flow of reality, the manifest nature of <u>that</u>, that the sense of 'I', the awareness of specific individuality, should be understood as being merely relative and so illusory. In the final analysis of the mind trained in the advanced meditative techniques taught in this book, the sense of 'I' is part of the illusion binding the mind to unenlightened behaviour. All individuality is merely an illusion appearing in the midst of conditions – the simple and absolute truth, insofar as it can be conveyed in words, is that we are all <u>that</u> alone, and nothing else.

At this stage in your travels along the path towards realisation of the final stage of enlightenment, having realised the psychological stage of enlightenment and not yet having spontaneously started samadhi, you need to learn how to act as an enlightened person. That is to say, to assist you in your inner development, you need a framework to guide and accustom you to enlightened forms of behaviour. It will be exactly as with the practices to raise the sexual energy described in chapter 5 of *The beginner's guide to enlightenment*: at first, compliance with these practices will be an act of determination and possibly imagination only; as your determination and practice improve, your inner experience will prepare you for the spontaneous beginning of samadhi.

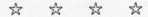

What are enlightened forms of behaviour?

The overcoming of your ignorance of the true nature of reality is your primary duty if you are seeking enlightenment. Overcoming ignorance both of <u>that</u>, and of the true nature of <u>this</u>, are, in the final analysis, the snuffing out of ignorance of one's own nature. Conditioned by space, time and karma, <u>that</u> works throughout your life to effect your freedom from the ignorance caused by self-imposed limitations.

Without exception, every thought and activity of an unenlightened person takes place in a fog of ignorance obscuring the true nature of each moment experienced. Once you have attained the fourth and final stage of enlightenment, you will have awoken from your ignorance, as you awaken from a dream realising that what passed before was only the product of the dreaming mind. Once enlightened, you will have the capacity to experience each moment just as it is, free from all burdens and free from all stress and sorrow.

Only by transcending the illusion that you have individual and separate existence can you succeed in transforming the ignorance and suffering of your mind in its conditioned state into the triumphant freedom and release from all burdens which are characteristic of mind in its fully enlightened state. This is a key feature of all fully developed Eastern or Western implicate technology systems. All models of reality which transcend the illusion of mere objectivity teach that, when understood in their true nature, the experiencer, the object of experience and the act of experiencing are one.

The key distinction between the enlightened and the unenlightened person is the enlightened person's realisation, based on direct experience, that the sense of 'I', the experience of separateness and individuality, is only relatively real and so is illusory and that the true and absolute nature of reality is an indivisible unity. Chapters 3 to 6 of this book teach a step-by-step method enabling you to break out of the ignorance of your true nature which binds you to suffering. The teachings in this chapter prepare you by encouraging you to adopt enlightened forms of thought and behaviour.

An enlightened person knows from experience that reacting to the needs and desires of the individual sense of 'I' leads only to entrapment in illusion. Acting on 'I want' and 'I need' brings only endless action and reaction within the self-balancing system governed by karma, which we experience as everyday life. Every activity based on an 'I' thought incurs either positive or negative karmic consequences and so perpetuates bondage to the illusion which sustains and underlies conditioned existence.

On the unshakeable authority of direct intuitive experience, the enlightened person knows that the obscuring fog of ignorance clears when the apparent separateness of all things is transcended. Acting from a level of being which transcends 'I' thoughts, the enlightened person functions as a conscious component of an inherently unified and harmonious system. All actions of a conscious component of reality are achieved without individual effort or volition and incur neutral karmic responses. The enlightened person experiences karma as a courteous and helpful guide through the unfolding of <u>this</u>, not as an implacable governing force dictating the events of one's life according to one's thoughts and actions.

The priceless benefits of enlightenment, a state of mind detached from pain, sorrow and all constraints of space and time, can only be realised through freedom from attachment. True freedom is freedom from attachment to any and all aspects of <u>this</u>, while accepting the inevitability of the processes of conditioned existence. Every enlightened person knows with utter certainty that only the body is born, ages, suffers and dies and only mind in its enlightened form is always free.

The enlightened person has learnt through experience to become detached from all things, from all of <u>this</u>, yet to look on <u>this</u> and its suffering people with infinite compassion. Even after enlightenment, you will still experience happiness and sorrow, success and failure, life and death – all the everyday experiences of ordinary life. To the enlightened mind, these are understood in their true nature – as stimuli which are experienced as part of <u>this</u>, and simultaneously known to be the manifest form of <u>that</u>.

Mind in its ever present nature is still, like an ocean without a wave, observing all things, including the thought process of each apparently individual mind. <u>That</u> manifests itself, experiences itself and witnesses itself as <u>this</u>. The enlightened person learns to experience <u>this</u>, all the variety of conditioned existence, with detached uninvolvement through freedom from attachment to stimuli.

As an unenlightened person struggling to attain enlightenment, you will have to learn to become detached from the constant stimuli bombarding your mind through your senses. Chapter 3 of this book teaches practical exercises which lead to enduring freedom from the urge to respond to stimuli. Committed daily practice of these meditative techniques will assist and guide you in your progress along the path.

Meditate long and hard on what it might mean to understand your individual experience as only being relatively real. Try to understand, through meditation, how you would behave if you no longer responded to the effects on your mind of the ten conditions. Try to understand that the bird flying free in the sky, the person in life who causes you the most aggravation and yourself, are equally important parts of a harmonious and integrated unity.

These Implicate Technology practical techniques for learning detachment from the influence of stimuli, offer the possibility for our Western cultures to make a significant advance. In the late-twentieth century, we in the West are poised to make the cultural leap from an ethically-based to a spiritually-based civilisation. To grasp the implications of this you will need to meditate on the evolutionary purpose of karma.

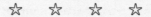

What is the evolutionary purpose of karma?

Karma embodies the purposive aspect of <u>this</u>. Karma functions as the teacher, providing balancing and correcting experiences to adjust the development of each person. The purpose of karma is to lead each person, at an appropriate pace and in appropriate circumstances, towards, and then along, a path leading to the final stage of enlightenment.

As your experience of the advanced meditative practices taught in this book unfolds, you will learn for yourself the evolutionary nature of karma. You will come to understand for yourself, through direct intuitive experience, the way your mind has been shaped to a single purpose – to break free of the illusion binding you to attachment to <u>this</u>. From examination of its contents, you will learn that your mind has been shaped in its development across lifetimes.

The experiences of each of us, accumulated across lifetimes, form a journey across an infinite sea of illusion. The journey ends not with death, which simply leads to another set of conditions, but with the realisation that <u>this</u> is <u>that</u>. Each incarnation you experience offers the opportunity to break out of the illusion that <u>this</u> is an objective reality, and to realise that in its true, final and absolute nature, <u>this</u> is a subjective reality.

Just as individuals grow and develop across and within lifetimes, so, too, do whole cultures. Cultures are vast aggregations of individual karma, shaped in turn by the wider karmic patterns of human history. Karma functions to offer cultures the chance to evolve, just as the same chance is constantly offered to individuals.

A clear, purposeful, evolutionary pattern can be seen in the devel-

25

opment of Western spiritual models of reality. This pattern can at last be perceived clearly, because of the unique conditions shaping our general Western cultural consciousness in the late-twentieth century. We in the West can look back with clarity on our spiritual history, because we are on the verge of an evolutionary leap forward in our spiritual development.

In comparison with the spiritual development of the Eastern cultures, we in the West have been developing, until now, at a much slower rate. For many thousands of years, great, spiritually-based cultures have risen, flowered and decayed in the East. These vastly different cultures – predominantly, but not exclusively, based on the Hindu, Buddhist and Taoist models of reality – have all reflected a profound understanding of the true nature of reality, variously expressed in terms appropriate to their several moral, social, political and economic environments.

In contrast, we in the West have developed more slowly from a primitive base of tribal religions, through the civilising influences of the Egyptian and Graeco-Roman cultures, past the unitive vision of Judaism to the great, ethically-based teachings of Christianity and Islam. This pattern of slow and steady growth reflects the sustained karmic conditioning and preparation of countless individuals, including you who are reading these words, across the experiences of many lifetimes. You have been carefully prepared, through the evolutionary purpose inherent in karma, for the role you will have to play in this lifetime, as our Western culture makes its transition from an ethically-based to a spiritually-based civilisation.

You have lived and gained experience, however slowly and unwillingly, and died many times in many different cultures. Evidence for the truth of this is contained in your own memory. Committed daily practice of the Implicate Technology meditative techniques taught in this book will release from your memory the skills, the experience and the inherent knowledge you will need to enable you to fulfil your role in the transformation of our culture, and will simultaneously assist you to progress towards achieving your full spiritual potential.

The Graeco-Roman cultural model of reality expressed a fragmented and relatively underdeveloped view of reality. The various gods and goddesses gave expression to the discrete and warring components of the individual mind. Only in the ancient Mystery model of reality did Graeco-Roman culture offer the committed individual the opportunity for a complete synthesis of the various aspects of mind, transcending the divisive schema of gods, goddesses and titans.

26

The fulfilment of individual and selfish aims was the end-product of the Graeco-Roman model of reality. The gods were offered sacrifices so that their powers might be invoked for human benefit. Without the benefit of an all-embracing and unifying vision of life, reality is experienced as devoid of coherent and purposeful meaning, subject to the chance whims of powers outside the control of the individual.

The unifying vision in general Western culture was introduced through the Jewish Old Testament model of reality. The *Shema*, the great Jewish prayer invoking the essential unity of reality, the first Western vision of monotheism, is expressed with succinctness and clarity: 'Hear, O Israel: The Lord our God, the Lord is One.' The experience of the inherent unity of all that exists which underlies the *Shema* is expressed in Implicate Technology terms as: 'There is only one reality. Reality is one.'

The Old Testament model of reality embodied the merciless face of karma: an eye for an eye, and a tooth for a tooth. The Western European scientific model of reality, produced over two thousand years later, reflected an equivalent level of understanding: to every action there is an equal and opposite reaction. The Jewish model of reality interprets the law of karma in a moral sense, and the scientific model interprets karma in a mechanistic sense – from the Implicate Technology perspective of a fully developed model of reality, these different formulations of a universal law merely reflect varied cultural approaches to the same level of understanding.

The Old Testament model of reality offers a coherent, if unforgiving, context in which to understand the experiences of life. Thousands of years later, the scientific model of reality is unable to offer even that much. The understanding which was once brilliant and clear becomes faded and obscure.

The next advance in the evolutionary development of Western consciousness lay with Christianity. The original Christian model of reality offered the opportunity to transcend the reactive nature of karma. Christianity introduced into Western consciousness an awareness of the paramount importance of forgiveness.

Through a genuine act of forgiveness, you can transcend, and so leave behind you, an accumulated weight of negative karma: this truth is expressed as religious implicate technology in the magnificently designed Lord's Prayer, and it is expressed as secular implicate technology in chapter 6 of *The beginner's guide to enlightenment*. The great contribution of Christianity to the evolution of Western cultural consciousness lay in its introduction of a teaching on the need for detachment from the instinctive response of 'an eye for an eye'. The ethical teachings of Christianity have had a far-reaching effect on the evolution of Western culture, as it moves slowly and painfully across the centuries towards a civilisation based on a fully-developed understanding of the spiritual nature of reality.

Christianity teaches the omnipresent nature of the kingdom of heaven, a realm whose nature cannot be communicated directly, only through parables. The original teaching of Jesus was structured to convey the experience of enlightenment to a simple, uneducated and temperamentally devout people. The experience of the ultimate nature of reality, which Jesus taught as the kingdom of heaven, finds its twentieth century equivalent in the Implicate Technology teaching that that can only be understood through direct experience, and cannot be conveyed in words.

The Graeco-Roman model of reality expressed a fragmented and divisive consciousness of this. The Jewish model, through a basic understanding of the reactive nature of karma, expressed a unified view of reality. The Christian model of reality, through the revelation that forgiveness can transcend the reactive nature of karma, reflected an advance in the level of Western consciousness.

The Implicate Technology meditative techniques taught in this book offer you the opportunity to take another evolutionary step forward in understanding the nature of reality. This teaching of the clear setting face to face with reality enables you to detach yourself from stimuli, your response to which binds you to the karmically reactive level of reality. Through becoming detached from stimuli in the midst of conditions, you learn to participate in the harmonious evolutionary flow of reality with the clear consciousness of the person whose mind has transcended the influence of karma.

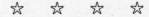

How do you become detached from stimuli in the midst of conditions?

Unlike the majority of its Eastern counterparts, this Western Implicate Technology model of reality teaches a coherent meditative system based entirely on the experiences of ordinary, everyday life. This chapter teaches you the overall context and chapter 3 teaches the practical techniques necessary to achieve detachment from the stimuli received by your mind at every moment. Once your mind has experienced its inherent stillness, witnessing each moment with detached serenity as it unfolds, you will be ready to begin the meditative practices leading to the final stage of enlightenment, as taught in chapters 4 to 6.

In general, Eastern implicate technology systems direct the mind to explore its nature through renouncing the stimuli of ordinary, day-to-day life. Out of a profound withdrawal from the attractions and distractions of everyday living, Eastern meditative systems develop an equally profound awareness of the true, final and absolute nature of reality. In this way, the Eastern implicate technologies have brought uncounted and uncountable numbers of seekers to the final stage of enlightenment.

Implicate Technology, a Western-originated, structured system of meditative disciplines, leads to an equivalent realisation of the nature of reality through embracing the stimuli of ordinary, day-to-day life. Out of profound absorption in, and then detachment from, the attractions and distractions of everyday life, Implicate Technology develops an equally profound awareness of the true, final and absolute nature of reality. In this way, this Western implicate technology can bring uncounted and uncountable numbers of seekers to the final stage of enlightenment.

Eastern and Western implicate technologies are simply two sides of the same coin. They approach the same goal from opposite perspectives. The differences merely reflect variations in cultural requirements according to the demands of place and time.

Chapter 3 of this book introduces the meditative practices leading to realisation of the mind's inherent stillness. You may be tempted to rush into these practices and to regard this chapter as interesting theory. That would be an error of judgement incurring compensating karmic consequences.

This chapter teaches you how to begin integrating every aspect of your life into the harmonious flow of reality. You will experience the compensating activity of karma as endless difficulties unless your mind and your life are in harmony with the way reality is moving. Meditate carefully on this chapter before proceeding with the practical exercises.

Reality is a unified, integrated process – every thought and every action incurs appropriate karmic responses. The way to transcend the karmically reactive system is to realise that the sense of 'I', the feeling and knowledge of your own individuality, is a relative perception and so lacks absolute reality. Chapter 3 begins the practical teaching which results in a shift in perception, from the relative and self-oriented sense of 'I' to the absolute awareness of <u>that</u>.

Unless you adjust your thoughts and actions to harmonise with the nature of reality, your efforts to practise the meditative techniques in chapter 3 will prove fruitless. You can only receive the gift of samadhi if you act in harmony with the flow of reality. That is to say, *if* **you think and behave in genuinely selfless and unselfish ways** *and* **you practise these meditative techniques,** *then* **you will spontaneously experience samadhi**.

<u>This</u> is an all-embracing, integrated unity – if you live selfishly, seeking to protect and enhance your own interests, you operate within the karmically reactive level of reality. Learn to accept what happens, regardless of your personal needs and desires. Learn to accept success and failure, gain and loss, praise and blame, with equal detachment. It is not you who lives, but <u>that</u> which lives you – learn to accept that the unchanging reality is that you can truly own nothing.

30

3   The path to a still mind

Mind in its unconditioned state is devoid of form or qualities – that is pure being, witnessing this as it unfolds. That in its conditioned state, individualised and absorbed in this, is engaged in ceaseless activity as a result of endless stimuli. Release from the bondage of conditioned existence comes through gaining detachment from stimuli.

☆   ☆   ☆   ☆

Why should you gain detachment from the endless stimuli of this?

That in its conditioned form, embodied in you who are reading these words, is entirely, and without possibility of exception, enmeshed in illusory perceptions of reality. The experience and understanding of reality gained through the five senses is only valid relative to the focus of perception. That is to say, your understanding of experience, based only on your five senses, is specific to yourself and so illusory. In the final analysis of the enlightened mind, all experience based only on sensual information is known to lead inevitably to suffering.

This understanding – that your experience of perceptible reality is an illusion – will only come once the illusion has been transcended, once you have awoken from your long sleep of ignorance of the nature of reality. The illusion can only be broken through attaining detachment from the incessant stimuli of perceptible reality. This chapter teaches the meditative practices which lead to detachment from stimuli and to the freedom and release of the mind in its enlightened state.

In its unenlightened form, your mind is continuously distracted from its inherent stillness by the apparently external and apparently objective nature of sensual stimuli. The unenlightened mind is deceived by the apparently external and objective nature of physical reality. You will transcend the illusion that reality consists of objective material phenom-

31

enon only when you have realised your mind's inherent stillness and quiescence.

Until this detachment from stimuli is realised, and you transcend the illusory nature of both the individual sense of 'I' and of objective reality, you will remain locked in the karmically reactive level of reality. That is to say, through the activity created by the interaction of karma with your thoughts and actions, you will remain bound to the endless cycle of birth, ageing, suffering and death. You will realise the final stage of enlightenment, from either a secular or a religious point of view, through practice, with unwavering determination, of the meditative techniques taught in this book. This will enable you to transcend stress, fear and suffering, and will bring, in their place, a genuine and lasting peace of mind transcending all conditions.

How do you prepare for the advanced meditative practices?

Begin by understanding that your goal is not merely to attain enlightenment for yourself, but to attain enlightenment so that, by teaching and by your own example, you can help others to attain its unparalleled benefits. We are all illusorily separate parts of an inherently unified whole, and the true value of your own attainment is measured by the assistance you give to others on the path.

Begin by understanding that the goal of this Implicate Technology meditative system, the attainment of the final stage of enlightenment, whether from a secular or a religious point of view, is a state of pure undistracted awareness. It is a state of mind concerned neither with past nor future; it simply witnesses and experiences the present moment. The mind, kept in its natural state of transcending all conditions, neither imagines, nor thinks, nor analyses, nor meditates, nor reflects.

Begin by understanding that everything you will learn about the nature of space, time and reality is already known to you. The process of recollecting lost knowledge, by practice of these meditative disciplines, is simply a matter of no longer forgetting what was once known. You sprang from <u>that</u>, you live now immersed in <u>this</u>, and you are set on the path to realising that you are now <u>that</u>, and have always and only been <u>that</u>.

Begin by understanding that you can meditate in virtually any and all circumstances. You can meditate while seated, walking, eating, making

32

love, working, resting or watching television – the list includes virtually every activity you engage in. The goal is realised when you live in meditation – that is to say, the goal is a state of meditation-enhanced awareness transcending any particular meditative practice.

Begin by selecting a readily available stimulus, which you can use to measure your progress in meditative detachment. The chosen stimulus can be aural or visual, or even tactile if you prefer – your aim is to realise detachment from stimuli through focusing your awareness on one simple, repetitive stimulus. You can use an inexpensive mechanical clock for a simple aural stimulus, or an inexpensive digital clock for a simple visual stimulus, or any other readily available stimulus.

How do I make the transition from the basic meditation to the advanced meditative practices?

Your experience in the periods before and after attaining the first stage of enlightenment was one of ever deepening understanding. To every question, it seemed you were given an answer. It was a time filled with wonder and meaning – a time when your inner awareness seemed to go through a total transformation.

Then, as the days and weeks became months, gradually and imperceptibly, at first, the rush of understanding slowed down. The days began to drag a little. One day you looked back and realised that somehow, without your quite noticing how or when, the sense of excitement, wonder and immanent, pulsating meaning had become dull, a faint echo of its original power.

Be comforted: this is all an important part of the process. Although it is unsatisfying to experience, your loss is more apparent than real. What has been happening is that the whole process, both your psychophysiological organism and conditioned existence, is delicately, and without overt indicators, re-aligning itself for the enormous transformations to come.

Accept as necessary this slow, unfulfilling period in your life. Realise that you still have the power to transform your understanding and your life. Then you are ready to begin the advanced meditative practices.

You have probably learnt, since attaining the first stage of enlightenment, that you are able to abandon the practice of counting the breaths during meditation. Until you gain familiarity with the advanced

33

meditative techniques, it will be best to restrict your practice of meditation to sitting in your favourite posture. At all times, during meditation, ensure that the teeth are lightly clenched and the tongue is touching the roof of the mouth.

Be clear: the full, final and absolute function of meditation is to realise and sustain a state of undistracted alertness. This is a state of mind free of, and transcending, the apparently endless tyranny of the thought process. This is true tranquillity of mind, when the mind's inherent stillness is realised through the mind abiding in its natural state.

From this point onwards, you must be completely committed to realising the fruits of meditation in your everyday life. Accept, without reservation or doubt, that there is no part of your life which is separate from the lessons you learn in meditation. If you forget this lesson, your spiritual efforts will prove fruitless.

Remember the lessons taught in *The beginner's guide to enlightenment*, chapter 6: you cannot progress in meditation while refusing to forgive someone who has wronged you or someone you love. You cannot progress along the spiritual path while pursuing selfish aims. You cannot move towards enlightenment by taking; progress in meditation can only be made through acts of inner giving.

☆   ☆   ☆   ☆

How is it possible to transcend the thought process?

Everything that you experience, each moment of every day, is the externalised and objectified thought process of the one, universal, all-embracing mind, which alone exists. Your own sense of specific individuality and separateness from all else that exists is an illusion based on ignorance of the true nature of reality. The path to attaining enlightenment is the process of breaking out of, or transcending, the illusion that this is an objective reality.

The true nature of mind, that is to say, the true nature of that, which is one and the same as the true nature of your own mind, is a qualityless, unconditioned awareness simultaneously incorporated in, and transcending, space, time and karma. For now, you will have to accept this as a received truth. In time, through sustained practice of the meditation techniques begun in this chapter, you will understand the truth of this through direct experience.

If you are following this meditative system from a religious point of view, realisation of that can be understood as realisation of God's love and as bliss in awareness of God. From the secular point of view of Implicate Technology, God is understood as the first manifestation of that in conditioned existence. From a religious context, that is understood as the Godhead, from which springs God, the source and object of all religious devotion.

It is purely a question of temperament whether you seek unity with God or realisation of that, mind in its unconditioned state. For some people, the religious path of devotion and surrender to God is the more meaningful; for others, this secular Implicate Technology path of knowledge of reality is the more attractive. It is six of one and half a dozen of the other—so choose a path according to your natural inclination. The most important activity in conditioned existence is to make progress along a spiritual path appropriate to your nature.

Your mind in its true nature is that; but at present it is shrouded in ignorance and sees only this. Diligent practice of the exercises begun in this chapter will progressively cleanse your mind of its ignorance. You once knew all that you are about to learn, but have forgotten it long, long ago.

The advanced meditative exercises in this chapter bring you to a realisation of the mind's inherent stillness and tranquillity. This is done by a graded series of exercises which develop your capacity to understand the workings of the thought process itself, as opposed to your current concern with its contents. Once you have become familiar with the process of thinking itself, you will be ready to begin the analysis of the nature of reality, as taught in chapter 4.

Do not attempt to rush through these exercises, and do not try to miss out any of them. Remember: to attain the gift of samadhi, you must live your life in harmony with the flow of reality, as taught in chapter 2.

As you practice the meditation, take care of your bodily needs. Eat simply, healthily and regularly. You will still have to fulfil your duties and obligations to those who are part of your life.

In time, when your understanding of the thought process is sufficiently developed, you will attain a stillness of mind, a natural tranquillity, which transcends the thought process. But before you can attain that spontaneous serenity, you must understand how, and with

35

what consequences, thoughts are formed. You begin by using thoughts to inhibit the process of thinking.

☆   ☆   ☆   ☆

How do you set about inhibiting the thought process itself?

The goal of this meditative exercise is to develop the skills enabling you to cut off a thought at the root, the very instant it rises up. This is a simple, but vital, skill. It is the first in a series of exercises leading to the development of a still mind.

The meditation is carried out as follows: you are sitting comfortably in your chosen position, alone, with your chosen stimulus. At every moment, thoughts arise as a result of stimuli. Your task is to cut off each thought in the very moment it arises.

Your mind is constantly exposed, through your five senses, to stimuli. As a result of these constant stimuli, thoughts occur continuously and endlessly. The purpose of this exercise is to give you the capacity to end, albeit temporarily, this apparently unceasing process.

Mind, in its conditioned state, is constantly distracted from its inherent stillness by the endless stimuli of this. This process of distraction is the root of the unenlightened mind's mistaken understanding that this is an objective reality. By learning to cut off a thought in its moment of formation, you begin the process of cleansing your mind of its accumulated ignorance of the true nature of this.

Before you realised the first stage of enlightenment, noise, sights and all forms of sensual experience were a severe form of distraction during your meditation. Now, as you move towards the second stage of enlightenment, the attainment of a still mind, what was once a source of difficulty, will become an aid, as you travel along the path. This is an experience you will find repeated many times.

The purpose of your chosen stimulus is to provide you with a simple and repetitive framework, against which you can test your progress. Whether you choose the ticking of a mechanical clock, or the passage of seconds on a digital clock, or any other simple and repetitive stimulus, your goal is to witness your chosen stimulus with a state of mind both transcending and embracing thought. The awareness of this transcending the limitations of thought is mind in its natural state.

To witness this from the qualityless and unconditioned perspective of that, or to witness this with the all-embracing compassion and love of

36

God, requires the ability to transcend the thought process. To realise the final stage of enlightenment, the birth of even a single thought must be prevented. To achieve the necessary inhibiting of the thought process itself requires considerable exercise of mental alertness.

Through the practice of these meditation exercises you will become trained in yogic disciplines to such a degree of alertness that you will be aware of the rise and fall of each thought. In time, you will be able to witness the flow of thoughts, rather than simply experience each thought as you do now. From that position of undistracted alertness you will learn to transcend the thought process.

First exercise

Begin your meditation practice: as soon as each thought crops up, try to cut it off at the root. Always try to bring your mind back to simply witnessing your chosen stimulus. When the next thought arises, repeat the process.

At first, this exercise will be very difficult to do, but with committed daily practice, it gradually becomes easier. All you are learning from this first exercise is that it is possible to cut off a thought at the root, at the very moment it arises.

This simple, but difficult, exercise should be continued outside of your formal practice of meditation. While engaged in any of your normal, everyday activities – at work, while travelling or eating, walking or watching television – continue your practice of cutting off thoughts as they arise. In this way, you will bring the fruits of meditation into every aspect of your life.

Through committed daily practice, you will become able to prolong the period of time during which you are able to make the effort to prevent thoughts arising. As a result of your efforts, you will become sensitised to one of the primary characteristics of the thought process. You will become aware that thoughts arise spontaneously, in a continuous and apparently endless stream.

Continue with this exercise until you feel adept at the instantaneous cutting off of a thought. A reasonable minimum length of time for this practice would be 2–4 weeks. You will gain nothing by attempting to hurry the process; become sensitive to your psycho-physiological system's capacity to learn, develop and unfold.

The purpose of this meditative exercise is achieved when you become aware of the stream of thoughts as both spontaneous and interminable.

You will not have achieved this awareness until you are able to observe the flow of thoughts with a tranquil detachment. This is an awareness in which you both experience and witness the flow of thoughts.

Once you have attained this tranquil detachment, even for the briefest of moments, you are ready to move on to the next exercise. As a result of this exercise, you will feel more aware than ever of the pressure of thoughts in your head—this is a good sign, indicating your growing sensitivity to the workings of the thought process. Now you are ready for the next exercise, learning not to react to thoughts.

How do you learn not to be distracted by your own thoughts?

The previous exercise taught you that thoughts arise spontaneously and flow in an apparently endless stream. Know that thoughts arise as a consequence of the stimuli your mind is constantly receiving through your body's five senses. As you have discovered from the previous exercise, the thought process can be stopped by an act of disciplined effort, but always the flow of thoughts begins again.

The previous exercise taught you that the flow of thoughts can only be temporarily stopped. This exercise begins the process of learning detachment from, and indifference to, the flow of your own thoughts. As your skill and experience becomes fully developed, through sustained and committed practice of these advanced Implicate Technology meditative practices, you will experience mind in its natural state: transcending all limitations of space, time and karma, you will witness, accept and understand all that unfolds, without attachment.

Second exercise
Begin your meditation practice: you are seated comfortably, alone and seeking to focus your awareness on your chosen stimulus. Your meditative task is to avoid interfering with any train of thought. Let the thoughts flow as they will, without shaping or directing them in any way, *and* at the same time try to be aware of your chosen stimulus.

Learn to be indifferent to the progress of your thoughts. Let your thoughts flow in their own pattern, without any interference from you.

Learn not to react to your own thoughts, and learn not to influence or impede them in any way.

This exercise is the opposite of the previous practice. In the first, you exercised with great strain to stop a thought in the moment of its birth. In this exercise, you maintain a relaxed, uninvolved alertness.

Through this practice of not reacting to thoughts, and simultaneously concentrating your awareness on the chosen stimulus, you are learning the rudiments of the art of witnessing this. As your skill with this technique develops, you will learn to extend the duration of the state of witnessing reality. You should expect to spend a minimum of 2–4 weeks at this exercise, remembering also to extend the lessons you learn to your everyday activities.

While inhibiting thoughts during the first exercise in this chapter, the mind when tensed became active and restless. During this second exercise, while you simply observe the flow of thoughts, the mind, being relaxed, assumes its natural shape of witnessing this. Your mind is a stubborn thing: it resists attempts to control it and works best when allowed to function in its natural way.

Mind in its natural state is an experience of undisturbed tranquillity. Thoughts are like waves rippling across a pond – purely surface activity. Like a deep pond, mind in its natural state is still, quiescent and at peace, presenting no barrier to the fish or the waves.

The purpose of this meditative exercise is to introduce you to the experience of mind in its natural state. Once you have experienced, even briefly, your mind's spontaneous and inherent stillness, you are ready to move on to the next exercise. Now, you will learn to extend the experience of inner stillness.

☆ ☆ ☆ ☆

How do you develop and extend the experience of mind in its natural state?

Committed daily practice of the previous meditative exercise will have introduced you, however remotely and briefly, to the experience of mind in its natural state – serene, still and transcending the thought process. This new exercise develops and strengthens your experience of the mind's inherent capability for inner stillness. This exercise utilises and combines the techniques learnt in the first two exercises.

These first three exercises are like an athlete's warm-up exercises. Just as an athlete would bend, stretch and flex the body muscles prior to an exercise session, so, in the same way, these preliminary yogic exercises loosen up and prepare your mind for the advanced training to come. These meditative exercises familiarise you with the limitations of the thought process, while simultaneously preparing you for the state of pure awareness which both transcends and embraces the thought process.

With great effort, you have learnt to cut off thoughts at the root, as they spontaneously and instantaneously come into being. With great patience, you have learnt to allow thoughts to flow uninterruptedly, as they spontaneously shape your experience of conditioned existence. Too much effort put into the first exercise created tiredness, both mental and physical, and only resulted in yet more thoughts; too much relaxation during the second exercise created lethargy, both mental and physical, and only resulted in absorption in the contents of your thought process.

This third exercise teaches you to maintain evenness of mind. The aim is to avoid the pitfalls both of intense straining for results, and of over-relaxing despite the need to remain alert. The goal of this exercise is to attain a middle course which avoids over-straining and over-relaxing and produces a state of relaxed alertness.

Third exercise

Begin your meditation practice: tense your mind to cut off thoughts as they arise; as soon as strain sets in, relax the mind and allow your thoughts to flow uninteruptedly. Continue this practice repeatedly – tense your mind and then relax it; tense your mind and then relax it. As you progress with the meditation, extend the time of practice into your ordinary, every-day activities.

When you can perform this process of tensing and relaxing alternately without giving much attention to the matter, you will have reached the goal of this exercise. Then you will have developed a steady, even awareness of the thought process itself. You will still be subject to thoughts – yet, simultaneously, you will be able to witness your thought process.

Once again, you should expect to spend a minimum of 2–4 weeks on this practice. Only through your own experience can you understand the point of these meditations. This understanding will come as your consciousness is expanded over a period of sustained practice.

At each stage, you can gauge, in a natural and easy way, when you are ready to move on to the next exercise. When you find your mind drawn to start the next exercise in the sequence, then you are ready to move on. Trust in your mind's inherent ability to move through the exercises at its own relaxed pace.

How do you transcend the thought process?

This fourth exercise gathers together, in one unified flowing movement, all the disparate strands of your understanding, your daily practice and the energies flowing through your psycho-physiological system. Success in this exercise opens up the possibility of living your life free from distractions, desire and suffering, and free from the dominance of the thought process—you become able to live your life as it occurs, now. The aim of this exercise is to produce the state of intense and sustained concentration which characterises the beginning of the process of samadhi.

As a result of your meditative practices up to this point, you will be keenly aware of the energy flowing in fits and starts around your psycho-physiological system. The cause and pattern of movement of this energy are described in the yoga of sexual energy, taught in chapter 5 of *The beginner's guide to enlightenment*. Your inherent sexual energy, referred to as *chi*, *prana* or *kundalini* in Eastern implicate technology systems, will have started to flow spontaneously, as a result of your advanced meditative practices.

Turn back now, and spend as much time as you need re-reading chapter 5 and meditating on the yoga of sexual energy. It is not essential for you to have practised the yogic techniques as taught in the first book. Either as a result of conscious practice of those techniques, or as an unconscious by-product of other meditations, your inherent psycho-physiological power source will have begun to flow naturally and spontaneously.

You may feel this energy as a tremendous source of power, coursing through your body and your mind. Sometimes, you feel overwhelmed by the energy and excitement coursing through you. Sometimes you feel drained and exhausted by the demands and strain being placed on both your mind and your body.

Chapter 5 of the first book in this structured, secular meditative system teaches the techniques for releasing the periodic build-up of energy. Be clear: the whole system of conditioned existence, the process involving your mind, body and the events of your life, is harmoniously and spontaneously self-balancing. Provided you set about meditating as taught in the context of a coherent, fully developed model of reality, there are no obstacles along the path to enlightenment which you cannot overcome.

The key to all meditative practices from this point onwards is maintaining undistracted alertness. Only through undistracted alertness can a yogically trained mind understand and experience the true nature of <u>this</u>. The path of undistractedness is the way of all enlightened people.

The key to maintaining undistracted alertness is to develop unwavering determination. Developing unwavering determination to maintain undistracted alertness is more important, at this stage, than success or failure. Above all, what will help you most is unwavering determination to keep practising until success comes, naturally and spontaneously.

Fourth exercise

Begin your meditation practice: keep your mind uncoupled from the thought process through unwavering determination to maintain undistracted alertness. Mind in its natural state transcends and witnesses the thought process, as being merely one of an infinite variety of objectified activities. Samadhi is the sustained experience of witnessing <u>this</u> from a state of mind transcending the limitations of the thought process.

The uncoupling of the mind from its thought process comes as a result of the mental strain caused by the previous meditative exercises. The extra effort demanded by this exercise creates the necessary tension and, with a sudden snap, so to speak, the mind becomes aware of its thought process as apparently separate and external. The mind just experiences thoughts as things of which it is aware – like the sound and feel of rain, voices near or in the distance, or the emotions felt on seeing a loved one.

The previous efforts to inhibit the thought process merely resulted in more thoughts. This fundamental experience of uncoupling the mind from the thought process resolves the problem by transcending it, by experiencing reality in a wider, more harmonious context. As you will learn in the remaining exercises, this initially raw, unstructured experience is gradually explored and refined to form the basis for enlightened understanding.

At first, your experience of the mind snapping free from all mental activity will be accompanied by the most intense period of concentration you will ever have encountered. The effort required to perform ordinary activities in a state of undistracted alertness is formidable. Be assured that the initial enormous drains of energy which are required to sustain this level of concentration will soon pass.

The essence of samadhi is undistracted awareness of what one is experiencing. In non-samadhic states of consciousness, the normal pattern of activity is the interpretation and understanding of sensual experiences by the thought process. In samadhic states of consciousness, that activity continues – but no longer as the sole or primary focus of awareness.

The task in samadhi is simply to be aware of what is happening. When you are sitting, walking or eating, in the state of samadhi, you are simply aware of sitting, walking or eating. At the same time, the thought process continues endlessly, but no longer is it the primary focus of your awareness.

If it helps you at first, simply lie down and devote all your energy to maintaining this simple degree of awareness. Equally, if it helps you, get up and walk around – your goal is to be aware, without succumbing to involvement in the contents of your thought process. What must not waver is your determination to maintain undistracted awareness; your ability to sustain undistracted awareness will undoubtedly waver at the beginning and for quite some time to come.

After the first, intense period of concentration is over, you may find yourself facing a different problem – boredom. Up to this point in your meditations, you will have derived great strength from the intensity of your inner experiences. As your consciousness expanded, through committed daily practice of the meditations, you began to understand the inherent richness and wonder of reality.

At this stage, as a result of intense meditative concentration, you are now able simply to witness and experience the current moment. At first, this is a rather bland experience. Put bluntly, sitting for sustained periods simply being aware of the surrounding environment, witnessing both inner and outer phenomena, can be very, very dull.

Instead of learning, understanding and growing each day, it seems now that you are devoting significant amounts of your energy to a state of witnessing which provides no inherent richness of experience. In

43

simpler language, at first samadhi seems to provide little in the way of results for the substantial effort put in. Be assured that this difficult, dull and unexciting period will pass as your awareness stabilizes in samadhic concentration.

Expect to spend a minimum of several weeks in a state of un-distracted, alert boredom. Just as a child does, by trial and error, you must learn to perform your ordinary, everyday activities. In a state of undistracted alertness you will rise from your bed, wash, eat your breakfast and perform your daily activities.

Trust in your intuition to guide you as you adjust to living with undistracted awareness. Rely on <u>Act</u> functioning automatically to guide you through each moment. If the pressure of events requires you to submit to the thought process, try to regain undistracted alertness as soon as you are able.

The reality is that with the birth of samadhic consciousness, you have entered into a fresh experience of life, entirely outside the bounds of ordinary consciousness. Working within this Implicate Technology framework, your growth will be rapid and more eventful, in terms of inner experience, than you can know at this stage. But first, your newly born samadhic awareness must become strongly rooted in your everyday experience of life.

Trust in your intuition to tell you when you are ready to move on to the next exercise. Rushing ahead too soon is foolish, and delaying too long before venturing into the unknown is wasteful. When you feel drawn to start the next exercise, *and* you feel relaxed and confident in your ability to sustain undistracted awareness, then move on.

Samadhi brings you the measureless benefit of being able to witness the world, detached from and transcending your own thought process. This detachment is the inherent stillness of mind in its natural state. Once you have become attuned to this inner stillness, you can explore, directly through your own experience, the full nature of reality.

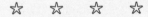

How do you attune yourself to the experience of mind un-coupled from involvement in thoughts?

As a result of successful completion of the previous meditative exercise, you have developed the capacity to enter into the state of mind known as samadhi. Be clear: you are, as yet, but a novice in the practice

44

of samadhi. You still have a long, long way to travel before your journey is ended – beyond yourself as an individual, beyond space, time and karma, beyond the restrictions of all conditions.

You have begun to experience the intrinsic emptiness and silence of the mind in its natural state. This is an experience of inner serenity which you will learn to enter and explore for longer and longer periods. Committed daily practice of the remaining exercises in this book will keep you on the well-trodden and reliable path to realisation of the final stage of enlightenment.

Over the next period of practice, you will come to realise just how far you have drifted from involvement in your everyday life. You will recognise that you have been unable to give your full attention to your ordinary life, owing to your intense efforts to control, to master and to transcend the thought process. Whatever consequences you have incurred as a result of this involuntary withdrawal are, as you well understand by now, the workings of karma in its balancing and harmonising aspects.

Banal as it may appear to be, the meditation taught in this section will bring you back to a full involvement in everyday life. As you will have come to expect by now, the meditation will be intensely demanding. What you may not expect is how clear, vivid, intense and all-absorbing you will find ordinary life, as a result of this meditation.

It is with this exercise that Implicate Technology diverges significantly, in terms of the results of its meditative practices, from the traditional Eastern models of reality. Within the frameworks of traditional spiritual systems, the start of samadhi heralds a period of ever-increasing withdrawal from everyday life; a withdrawal into an intensely and exclusively inward contemplation of the transcendental nature of reality. This results in an intermediate stage of consciousness, often mistaken for the final stage of enlightenment, which is characterised by the temporary ability to understand the transcendental nature of reality – and accompanied by the temporary absence of body-consciousness.

Such experiences, involving as they do temporary loss of awareness through the senses, and the temporary loss of the ability to function in the world, have no place in our busy, pressurised Western cultures. Consider the implications of explaining to your boss that your work is late because you were in a profound meditative trance. How could you meet your everyday commitments when, at any time, you might slip into a profound state of meditative unconsciousness of the world?

Eastern meditative systems teach how to realise the transcendental nature of reality – that the world is the product of the one mind – through renouncing everyday life. This Western meditative system teaches the realisation of the transcendental nature of reality – that this is that – through embracing everyday life. The same eternal truth is taught in both cases; only the outer form of the path varies according to the cultural needs of place and time.

This Western model of reality directs the meditator's attention simultaneously inwards towards realising the transcendental nature of this, and outwards towards witnessing and participating in ordinary, everyday life. Implicate Technology teaches a path involving the constant intertwining of everyday life with the growing understanding of the inherently transcendental nature of that life. Implicate Technology teaches, through meditative practices based on the experiences of ordinary life, that this and that are one and the same.

As a result of this process of balancing inner development and outer involvement, the loss of bodily awareness, and the consequent temporary inability to function in ordinary life, are avoided. The meditator continuously interacts with, and learns from, the immediate cultural environment. Through constantly balancing and harmonising inner awareness and outer activity, the process of samadhic consciousness is experienced with ever-increasing alertness – the world is witnessed, and acted in, with an ever-growing awareness of its true and transcendental nature.

The technique used for this meditative exercise is to practise detachment from rich and varied stimuli by keeping awareness uncoupled from your thought process. This fifth exercise is simply an extended form of the previous meditative technique. Committed daily practice will extend and strengthen your capacity to sustain samadhi.

The material for this meditation is your ordinary environment. According to your personal taste, choose a suitable source of stimuli as the basis for meditation. This source can be anything, so long as it is readily available to you – television, radio, cinema, music, watching what goes on in the street.

Fifth exercise

Begin your meditation practice: choose a rich, varied and easily accessible source of stimuli. Witness your chosen stimuli with an intense, keen alertness. Simultaneously, keep your

**awareness located in the stillness of samadhi, not in your
thought process.**

Witness your chosen source of stimuli without participating. That is
to say, become absorbed in what is presented to you, but avoid
distraction through becoming absorbed in the contents of your thoughts.
Practice observing <u>this</u>, in all its richness and variety, with undistracted
alertness, while remaining detached from any of the stimuli you
experience.

As a result of your sustained efforts in this meditation, the inherent
sexual energy flowing round your system will spontaneously and
harmoniously settle down. The great surges of unrefined energy you
have been experiencing will channel themselves into the body's natural,
self-balancing energy system. This energy system can be formally
studied through the teachings on *prana* or *chi* to be found in Eastern
implicate technology systems; or you can allow nature to take its course
while you concentrate on your meditation.

The inherent implicate energy, flowing spontaneously into its natural
channels through practice of this exercise, brings with it experiences
entirely outside the range of normal consciousness. You will probably be
hungry for these as proof of your advancement, and as evidence of the
truth of some particular view of reality which you cherish. All such
attitudes are impediments on the path, and must be outgrown through
sustained committed practice of meditation.

The most common form of supernormal experience is to have visions.
Visions are seen with the inner eye and heard with the inner ear, in a
manner of speaking. Visions can encompass any aspect of <u>this</u>, past or
present or future.

Be clear: visions are neither enlightenment nor an experience of
universal truth. Visions are simply another experience along the way,
and properly understood they can be of great value to you in understanding the nature of reality. Like any other aspect of <u>this</u>, visions are
part of the educational and enlightening process which <u>this</u> truly is.

Be very cautious in talking to others about your visions. As a culture,
we in the West know little of such experiences. We know even less how to
derive benefit from the visionary experience.

Visions are best understood as a spontaneously occurring self-tuition
course on aspects of reality relevant to the development of the experiencer. Your visions will probably occur as a self-refining series of
spontaneous image/experiences. They will draw your attention to an

aspect of reality, that is to say they will teach you about an aspect of your own nature, which you need to understand before you can proceed along the path.

Neither inhibit nor encourage whatever supernormal image/experiences may arise. Be neither glad nor afraid, however pleasant or unpleasant these experiences may be. Simply witness the vision, the complex of inner image and experience, without participating – and so extend your experience of samadhi.

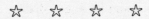

What is the outcome of a sustained period of undistracted witnessing of stimuli as they occur?

Through sustained practice of samadhi, your psycho-physiological system will spontaneously re-align and re-balance its energy flows. Your body will become calmer, your sleep pattern will be less disturbed, and you will learn to recognise your thought process as simply another phenomenon occurring as part of <u>this</u>. You will learn to recognise that thoughts occur in the mind as a result of stimuli, and that the mind and thoughts are not identical.

For the moment, as a result of your practice of the previous exercises, you have trained your mind to a state of intense alertness. You are now so keenly aware of the relationship between thoughts and stimuli that, sometimes, <u>this</u> seems overwhelming. Just as you experienced an apparent instability in conditions before realising the first stage of enlightenment, you may undergo a similar experience at this stage as a temporary function of your heightened sensitivity to the effects of stimuli.

When the awareness is focused through the intrinsic emptiness and silence of samadhi, the mind experiences stimuli as the rising and falling away of thoughts. When distracted, and so absorbed in the flow of thoughts, the mind loses awareness of its inherent stillness. The key to the next exercise is to keep the mind still, by remaining unresponsive to the endless interplay of stimulus and thought-response.

Sixth exercise
During samadhi, the state of awareness transcending and encompassing the thought process, one becomes conscious of thoughts the instant they arise. Trained to an extraordinary

degree of alertness by these advanced meditative practices, your mind has developed the ability to be aware instantly of the birth of a thought, and the ability to inhibit the development of any train of thought. This practice of inhibiting thoughts at birth, in the instant they arise, should be sustained until, quite naturally and spontaneously, you become indifferent and unresponsive to the rising and passing away of thoughts.

When you have been successful in this meditation, you will be able, without great effort, to maintain your mind in its natural state – still, serene and inherently devoid of thoughts. Thoughts will still occur in your mind; but now, you will be able to treat them with the same detachment with which you view the scene passing outside the windows of a train on a long journey. You will experience the thought process as an endless flow of stimuli, and you will simultaneously transcend the thought process through realising the inherent emptiness and stillness of your mind.

You will become capable of living the ordinary, everyday events of your life while both fully participating in these events, and silently, serenely witnessing the events, both inner and outer. The ability to witness <u>this</u>, including your own thought process, without inhibition or reaction will occur effortlessly and spontaneously. The state of still, thought-free witnessing is a continuous, unbroken consciousness that <u>this</u> comprises physical and mental stimuli.

In samadhi, the ability to recognise and transcend your mind's instinctive reactions to the stimuli of <u>this</u> is an essential precondition for breaking free of the illusion that <u>this</u> is an objective reality comprising separate people, places and things. Only the mind in its natural state, calm and free of thoughts, can undertake the task of exploring and transcending the nature of space and time. Characteristic of deepest samadhi is the ability to witness <u>this</u> with the serene, unfailing acceptance of what is.

The remaining Implicate Technology meditative practices will bring you to realisation of the absolute truth about your original and ever-present nature. In the moment of knowing the truth, your mind will become free – beyond time, space, karma and the constraints of life and death. To achieve this, all you have to do is continue with committed daily practice of meditation as instructed.

49

What is the second stage of enlightenment?

By actual realisation, through your own experience, of the mind's inherent stillness, you have attained the second stage of enlightenment. The purpose of this section is to round out your experience and to point out the way ahead. You may choose to rest at this point on your journey, or you may find youself proceeding with the exploration of reality, as taught in chapter 4.

You have realised the mind in its natural state – settled, serene and utterly still. This is an experience of unparalleled ordinariness. It is quite unremarkable because it is simply the <u>Act</u> of witnessing <u>this</u>.

The ancient and time-honoured simile for the mind in its natural state cannot be surpassed for its accuracy of description. **The mind in its natural state is calm and still, like an ocean without a wave**. You have won the right to live the rest of your life in a sea of serenity.

As you have discovered from your own experience, thoughts still occur endlessly while the mind is in its natural state. Through meditation you have developed the ability to be indifferent to the rise and fall of the mind's impressions. Having realised the mind's inherent stillness, you are indifferent to the movement of thoughts.

Your mind is now capable of discriminating between reality as experienced through the limitations of the individual sense of 'I', and that same reality as experienced through the absence of the sense of 'I'. Up to this point in your meditations, you have lived, loved and worked on the inherently illusory basis that the individual sense of 'I' is the natural focus through which <u>this</u> is experienced. The exercises taught in the next chapter will awaken your mind's inherent ability to experience <u>this</u> through the absence of the illusory individual sense of 'I'.

The transpersonal explorations of the nature of reality, which begin in chapter 4, utilise one-pointedness of mind. A one-pointed mind is capable of meditating on one thought at a time for as extended a period of time as is necessary until understanding develops. Through developing this ability, the true, final and absolute nature of reality will become irrevocably known to you.

The true nature of <u>this</u> is that it is the externalised and objectified thought process of the one, unified, all-embracing, transcendent mind. Your relative and illusory individual sense of 'I', is an inseparable component of <u>that</u>. The purpose of the meditative system taught in

50

this book is to consciously re-unite you with <u>that</u>, and so enable you to know each thing separately and yet simultaneously to know all things as one.

4 The path to the realisation of _that_

This is _that_, and only _that_. _This_ is the constantly unfolding, illusorily objective thought process of the one, universal, all-embracing mind. By structured meditation on the nature of _this_, using the ever simpler perceptions of the mind in its still and natural state, you come at last to understand that _this_ is _that_.

4.1 The transcending of individuality

What is the illusory nature of individual experience?

As you will soon learn if the lesson is not already clear, language at best is only a crude pointer to the nature of reality. In comparison with direct intuitive experience, spiritually barren, late-twentieth century language is dull and clumsy. Yet, despite its limitations, language is the best available tool in the late-twentieth century by which the understanding of the true nature of _this_ may be spread.

There is not now, nor has there been or ever can there be, any such thing as two unrelated individuals or events. All distinctions of time and space are relative to the consciousness which experiences them, and so are illusory from the absolute perspective of mind in its fully enlightened state. 'I' who write these words and 'you' who read them can simultaneously be relative points of reference for experiencing _this_, and absolute witnesses of _this_ as _that_.

The simultaneous experiencing of _this_ as relative and so illusory, and as the manifest form of _that_ and so absolute and real, can only be described in language which is blatantly contradictory. The limitations lie in language, not in reality. 'You', who have no absolute existence, can experience _this_ simultaneously both in its relative nature as _this_ and in its absolute nature as _that_.

By virtue of having attained a still, settled and silent mind, through successful completion of the exercises in chapter 3, you are poised to transcend the relative, and so illusory, sense of individuality. Successful completion of the first set of exercises in this chapter will enable you to transcend the illusion of your individual existence. Through your own hard work and your own insights, you will come to understand through experience that 'you' and 'I' are merely the result of the superficial play of illusion obscuring the true nature of <u>this</u>.

Language cannot express the transcendent experience of reality simultaneously in its absolute and relative forms. As you proceed along the path, be directed by your intuitive experiences, and do not waste your time attempting to resolve the contradictions by intellectual methods. Reality transcends all intellectual theories, and your task is to experience reality in its true nature, beyond mere words, thoughts or theories.

The illusory nature of individual experience is realised through one-pointed meditation. By virtue of having realised the mind in its natural state, you are now capable of one-pointed meditation. Simply meditate as instructed.

One-pointed meditation is conducted by the simultaneous processes of holding fast to the stillness of samadhi and so maintaining continuous undistracted alertness, and of continuing with the process of meditative reflection and analysis. Your mind is now capable of dwelling on one thought at a time for sustained periods. Maintain stillness of mind and simultaneously meditate as directed in a one-pointed manner.

In this part of chapter 4, you are given a series of questions on which to meditate in a one-pointed manner. **Holding fast to undistracted awareness, indifferent to the rising and falling away of thoughts, you will simultaneously repeat each question over and over in your mind, for as long as necessary**. Each exercise can be successfully completed in a minimum of a day, or it could take a week, a year or a lifetime.

The amount of time you need to spend on each question is a function of the quality and amount of effort you put into the meditation. It is pointless trying to move on before you have developed a deep-rooted intuitive understanding of the reality behind each answer. **When your intuition enables you to understand the answer provided, then and only then should you move on to the next question.**

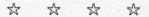

What are the meditative practices for transcending the illusion of individuality?

Committed one-pointed practice of the exercises in this section establishes the ability to distinguish between the individual sense of 'I', the small and relative part of mind in which thoughts occur, and the absence of the individual sense of 'I', the absolute mind transcending the thought process. Our Western educational systems endeavour to bring a child to maturity with a well developed sense of individuality. In contrast, through these advanced meditative exercises, you will learn that 'I'-oriented awareness is a cripplingly limited and confining way to experience reality.

The illusory, subjective sense of 'I' is the basis for the wrong understanding that <u>this</u> is an objective reality. Put simply, common-sense wrongly tells you that 'I', 'you' and this book are three clearly separate things. It is essential to transcend the individual sense of 'I' through meditation if you are to break out of the illusion that there is now, or ever could be, separate and unconnected people, things or events.

In reality, all perceptions of difference and experience of separateness are merely the superficial result of misunderstanding the nature of the ten conditions. All people, events and things – all that is, has been or can be – are, in the final analysis of the enlightened mind, superficial variations in manifestation of the one, formless, qualityless, universal and all-embracing mind. These Implicate Technology teachings of the clear setting face-to-face with reality have only one result – the re-uniting of the individual consciousness with <u>that</u>, its original nature.

All individual and cultural aims, achievements and experiences are simply evolutionary steps along the path to re-unite <u>this</u> with <u>that</u>. Some times are warmer, some are cooler; all times are movement towards realisation of <u>that</u>, obscured by the play of the ten conditions. Your conscious contribution towards this vast evolutionary goal begins with understanding, through direct intuitive experience, that 'I' and 'objective reality' are two apparent opposites which in reality are different aspects of the same unity, locked in an eternal illusion of separateness.

The goal of this part of the teaching will be realised when you know with the certainty of your own experience that the meditator, the object of meditation and the act of meditating are one. The observer, the thing observed and the act of observation are inseparable. The meditator, who is yourself, simply cannot be found when sought in the disciplined manner taught here.

Unenlightened Western scientists, groping in the dark (that is to say, lacking a coherent and structured model of reality) with enormously expensive technology and years of training and experience, have established through experiments that the observer, the thing observed and the act of observation are inseparable. You, alone in meditation, can establish the same truth about the nature of reality with a far greater authority of understanding. Our vastly expensive Western explicate science provides no conclusions or insights into the nature of reality which cannot be reached with greater understanding and insight by the individual using the tools of the world's many implicate technologies.

How do 'I' meditate in a one-pointed manner?

By successfully completing the exercises in chapter 3, you have developed the capacity to experience the inherent peace and stillness of mind in its natural state. This is a state of pure awareness, transcending and embracing the thought process. You are now going to learn how to use the thought process to explore the nature of reality, while retaining awareness of the mind's inherent stillness.

This you can do because you have developed the ability to bring the mind to a single focus. You are now able to focus your awareness on one object for sustained periods. After a sufficient period of sustained one-pointed meditation on each object, your intuition will provide you with a direct understanding of the true nature of each object of meditation.

The first set of objects for your meditation are a series of questions. Tackle them patiently, one by one in the order given. Do not proceed to meditate on the next question until you understand with intuitive certainty the current object of your meditation.

Do not be tempted to rush these exercises. They will teach you the true nature of individual experience. Allow the process whereby 'your' mind remembers its own nature to unfold at its own pace.

One-pointed meditation is conducted in two stages. When you have mastered the first stage, you will find your awareness moving spontaneously on to the second stage. Simply let the process unfold in its own way and in its own time.

The first stage of absorption in one-pointed meditation is when awareness is focused on the outer form of the object. That is to say, one experiences an unwavering concentration on the object, while at the same time thoughts about the object rise and fall in awareness. Although these thoughts can reflect any aspect of the object, they are irrelevant distractions and awareness should not be allowed to settle on any particular thought.

The second stage of absorption in one-pointed meditation is when awareness is focused on the inner form of the object. That is to say, one experiences an unwavering and undistracted concentration on the object. When the mind is settled and still, awareness moves from the distractions of the thought process to direct intuitive experience of the object itself.

How do 'I' begin the meditative process of distinguishing between <u>this</u> as understood through the limiting and illusory sense of 'I' and <u>this</u> experienced directly through the absence of the sense of 'I'?

To assist you in this process, the first meditation of this set will be discussed in detail. Once you have successfully experienced this first one-pointed meditation, you will find that the others follow the same pattern. Be clear: you are not engaged in a process of accumulating information or facts about the nature of reality – rather, you are learning to experience <u>this</u> in an increasingly simple, direct and intuitive way.

What is the real nature of mind in its still and natural state? The real nature of mind is extension through space. That is to say, space and the objects it contains are products of mind.

The paragraph above is the object of your meditation. More precisely, the question in **bold** print is to be the focus of your one-pointed awareness. When you have completed this meditation you will know, with the clarity and certainty of direct intuitive experience, that the answer provided reflects the nature of reality.

This meditation is the first of a graded series of exercises designed to awaken your mind's inherent ability to experience the transcendental nature of reality. The simple truth is that all you are now learning by direct intuitive experience was once known to you without any obscuring ignorance. Through time and the accumulated weight of experience across lifetimes, you lost sight of the inherent unity of <u>this</u>, and in your growing ignorance fell into the illusion that reality consists of objective, material phenomena. Now you are ready to work at the conscious process of recollecting your true nature, which transcends space, time, karma and all the other conditions which limit and determine the events of your life.

Begin this meditation by focusing your awareness one-pointedly on the question printed above in **bold** type. You will find that quite spontaneously your mind keeps repeating the question, over and over and over. After a time, you will find it requires relatively little effort to sustain awareness of this constant repetition.

In the first stage of absorption in one-pointed meditation, several processes occur simultaneously. These processes include both inner and outer activities. Your task is to engage in all activities required of you, while repeating one-pointedly the question printed in **bold**.

The inner activities are based on the thoughts generated by your one-pointed concentration on the object of meditation. A host of questions and observations will arise in your mind. You will attempt to understand your meditation in terms of the contents of your thought process.

All this activity is fruitless, and cannot take you further along the path of understanding the nature of reality through direct intuitive experience. Instead of putting your energy into thinking, practise whatever skills you have developed in performing the meditations from chapter 3 to still the thought process. Your real task is to focus one-pointedly on the **bold** question, and simultaneously to detach your awareness from absorption in the rising and falling away of your mind's impressions.

The outer activities are the events of your day, configured by karma. You still have to get up, brush your teeth, eat, talk to other people and engage in whatever activities the day presents you with. In this secular Implicate Technology teaching, one-pointed meditation is conducted in the midst of ordinary, everyday conditions.

After a time, it should become clear to you that although one-pointed meditation is a new experience, the ability to detach your mind from responding to stimuli, both inner and outer, is familiar. You are able to practise one-pointed meditation because your efforts in the meditations of chapter 3 produced a still mind. The first stage of one-pointed absorption comes to a close when you are able to focus on the object of meditation exclusively *and* your mind becomes still and serene through detachment from stimuli.

57

The second stage of one-pointed meditation is characterised by the mind becoming quiet enough to be absorbed in the object of attention. Your mind will be serene and still, observing the constant repetition of the **bold** question *and* not responding to whatever thoughts may arise from inner and outer stimuli. From this serene, one-pointed concentration comes understanding based on direct experience of the object of meditation.

When the mind is absorbed in the object of attention, experience of the object's true nature arises and unfolds from pure, direct, clear intuition. The end result of your sustained effort will be surprisingly simple and obvious. You will just understand that the answer given reflects the nature of reality.

Of course, this understanding is not possible through a mere intellectual appreciation. In this particular meditation, you will know, with the unshakeable certainty of direct intuitive experience, that the nature of mind in its natural state is extension through space. When this happens, don't waste your time trying to make logical sense of the experience – eat a satisfying meal, have a relaxing bath and a good night's rest, and then start on the following meditation.

How do 'I' complete the process of realising that the observer, the thing observed and the act of observation are one?

Before proceeding with the remaining exercises in this set, you would do well to pause and take stock of your situation. When this set of exercises is successfully completed, you will have transcended the illusion of individual and separate existence. When you have realised that truth, working just with these teachings and your own life as the raw materials, you will have travelled further in the understanding of reality than has been attained by our most advanced late-twentieth century Western science.

It is very easy for your mind to get carried away by exhilaration and excitement – soon your insights into the nature of reality will far transcend anything an explicate, materially-based science can teach. You may be tempted to feel that you are an exceptional person, developing extraordinary insights and abilities. What enjoyment, what power, what recognition you can see in your mind's eye awaits you.

Simply pay no attention to such stimuli. Through the workings of karma, reality still configures itself to test your capacity for detachment from stimuli. At all times, you must maintain undistracted alertness to ensure that you are not diverted from the path to the final, transcendental stage of enlightenment.

One-pointed meditation requires that you deal simply, clearly and directly with what is in front of you. Throughout your life, Live and Act. Always and only, bring your awareness back to undistracted contemplation of, and undistracted involvement in, the present moment.

Carried out as instructed above, the remaining meditations in this set will gradually reveal to you the true nature of mental activity. By careful contemplation and analysis, you will search for who it is who is doing the contemplating, analysing and searching. When sought with undistracted alertness and unwavering awareness of the mind's natural stillness, it will be discovered that the seeker cannot be found.

How does mind remain still and serene? Simply by taking its natural shape – extension through space. When relaxed, the yogically trained mind becomes still.

How does mind move from its natural serenity and stillness? Through reaction to stimuli, both internal and external. The significance of the yogic techniques you learned in chapter 3 should now be clear to you – they enable the inverse process.

When the mind responds to stimuli, does it also remain still? All mental activity of thoughts, emotions and observations can occur simultaneously with awareness located in the still state. The state of still, serene witnessing embraces and transcends reactions to stimuli.

When awareness is located in the mind's natural serenity and stillness, does the mind respond to stimuli? Calm, clear and filled with delight, mind in its natural state is indifferent to stimuli and the reactions they cause. The still mind is not distracted from its serenity by the stimuli it experiences.

Is the mind in its natural state, still and free from mental activity, different from the mind which experiences mental activity? That component of mind which experiences mental activity is what you have mistakenly, all your life, assumed to be the irreducible focus of experience – the individual sense of 'I'. Mind in its natural state is a state of awareness in which each individual mind, each unique sense of 'I', is intuitively known in its true form as a confined component, a mere fraction of the true potential of mind.

Mind in its still form and mind in its active form are only apparently polar opposites. That limited component of mind which experiences mental activity on the one hand, and the expanded serene awareness of mind in its natural state on the other, are respectively gross and subtle forms of awareness. The active component of mind and the still component are simply gradations, or variations in form, of the one, universal, all-embracing, transcendent mind.

What is the real nature of mind in its active form, the individual sense of 'I'? Mind in its gross form, the complex of thoughts and emotions comprising the individual sense of 'I', is a densely structured system of conditioned responses to stimuli. When awareness operates in that context, the ultimately non-existent 'I'-consciousness is intimately and irrevocably bound up in the karmically reactive system, which results in rebirth after rebirth.

The sense of 'I', or 'I'-consciousness, all the attributes of mind and personality which comprise each unique individual, is a specific and limited structure of mental activity located at a particular point in space and time. Each individual consciousness is a unique viewpoint, a special window on conditioned existence. There are infinitely many ways to experience this.

Consider this image: you can only see clearly what is on the other side of a window if the window itself is clear. The heat of activity generated by the reaction between the individual sense of 'I' and the endless stimuli of this creates an obscuring condensation on each individual window on this. Consciousness working within the limitations of mind in its active and individual form, in other words the ordinary un-enlightened person, cannot under any circumstances perceive this clearly, as it is.

As you have learned from your advanced meditative practices, consciousness can move from a focus of awareness located in mind in its active form, to a focus of experience located in mind in its still and natural shape. As the mind becomes indifferent to the endless stimuli of conditioned existence, the heat generated by mental activity gradually reduces. As the condensation on the window of perception gradually clears, the true nature of reality becomes apparent.

How does mind in its active form become mind in its natural, serene form? There is no absolute distinction or point of demarcation, between mind in its active and mind in its still forms. They are simply gross and subtle forms of the one, all-embracing, unified and transcendent mind, <u>that</u>.

In the previous exercise, you analysed the nature of active mind from the viewpoint of mind in its serene, still and natural state. When you search for the central, real and unshakeable core of individual experience, you discover only mind in its still and impersonal form. Mind in its individual and active form, when sought in a yogically disciplined way, cannot be found.

The observer, mind in its still and impersonal form, and the thing observed, mind in its active individual form, are found through experience to be inseparable. The inseparability of the observer, the thing observed and the act of observing is an irreducible central experience of any advanced meditative practice. This unshakeable truth of reality is knowable only by direct intuitive experience – the intellect, unaided by meditation-enhanced intuition, cannot encompass or explain this fundamental truth.

Be clear: it is not 'I' who experiences <u>this</u>. It is <u>that</u> which experiences through the individual sense of 'I'. It is not 'I' who lives, but <u>that</u> which lives us.

By searching diligently and with undistracted awareness, or mindfulness as it is known in Buddhist implicate technology, for who it is who is doing the meditating and searching, you have discovered not the core of your individuality but an impersonal stillness and serenity. The object of meditation has been found to be inseparable from the meditator, who is inseparable from the act of meditation. As a careful inspection of the literature of the East on advanced meditative practices will reveal, regardless of the object of meditation chosen, it is invariably found to merge into an intuitive experience of reality as an inseparable, coherent, integrated and purposeful unity.

Through this realisation of the inseparability of reality, you now understand with direct intuitive experience that all aspects of mind form a meaningful whole. You have also learned that the meditator, when sought, cannot be found. The remainder of this Implicate Technology structured meditative system will bring you to the understanding that these insights reflect fundamental laws describing the underlying implicate structure of reality.

61

The first of these laws, understandable fully only when the final stage of enlightenment has been realised, is that every aspect of this is an externalised thought product of that. The second of these laws is that all sense of individuality, loneliness and separateness is an illusion suffered by mind in its unenlightened state. Motivated by unbounded love and compassion, the enlightened person works endlessly to bring all others to the release and freedom of enlightenment.

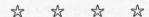

4.2 The awakening of transcendent consciousness

What is the meditative practice for allowing the mind's transcendental nature to unfold?

The previous, intense, phase of exploration and analysis has been completed. Patient, consistent practice in one-pointed meditation has revealed that the meditator cannot be found. The nature of mind has been explored, through direct intuitive experience, and the illusion of individuality has been transcended.

You have learned to distinguish between mind in its active individual state and mind in its still natural state. You have intuited that the two apparently opposite states are simply different forms of the one mind. Now you will learn to direct your efforts towards realising that, mind in its transcendental all-embracing state.

Up to this meditative practice, you have been exploring the nature of this, conditioned existence. Your journey has been relentlessly inwards, establishing the forms and characteristics of the deepest and simplest states of mind. From this exercise onwards, you will explore the nature of that, mind in its unconditioned state; or, if you are religiously inclined, you can use these exercises to apprehend the nature and being of God.

The remaining exercises in this chapter will help you to realise that. Through direct intuitive experience, they will teach you that this is that. If you are practising these exercises within the context of a religious model of reality, you will realise that the world is the manifest form of God.

Successful completion of the exercises in this chapter marks a profound turning about in your mind. Irrevocably, your mind will move to a transcendentally based awareness. Simply, clearly and directly, you will experience <u>this</u> in its true nature as <u>that</u>.

What is the illusory nature of all activity of the mind?

The meditative practice for allowing transcendental awareness to unfold is, yet again, simplicity itself. **Whatever thoughts, ideas or emotions arise, neither inhibit nor encourage – simply observe**. If this practice is carried out as instructed, the illusory nature of mental activity will be realised.

Your mind has now been trained to a degree of extraordinary alertness. It is capable of recognising the moment of birth of each thought, emotion or idea. All that is required at this stage is that whatever arises in your mind be allowed to do so freely, without any interference from you – simply be aware of each moment's mental activity without becoming involved.

This exercise develops your capacity to witness <u>this</u> with detachment. This is not the detachment born of insensitivity to self and others. This is the serenity and detachment of mind in its true state, witnessing its own mental activities.

First, you will learn to recognise your own mental products and activities in their illusory nature. Then you will learn that all aspects of <u>this</u> are the products and activities of <u>that</u>, the transcendent universal mind. Finally, your mental processes will re-integrate with <u>that</u>; and with the clarity, wisdom and delight in what is, which is characteristic of <u>that</u>, you will observe the unfolding of the conditioned thought process which is <u>this</u>.

If you establish a simple and supportive meditative framework, it will assist you in the process of detached witnessing of your own thought process. A simple and supportive meditative framework is supplied by one-pointed awareness of the mechanical ticking of a clock. Alternatively, you can utilise the constant noises, loud or slight, which occur in everyday life – a person with an aural handicap should substitute a simple, repetitive visual stimulus, such as the passage of seconds on a digital watch.

The technique is to focus awareness one-pointedly on the chosen stimulus. Become aware, for sustained periods, of the aural or visual

63

stimulus as the wider or primary context. Realise that your mind's inner activities, arising and falling away with each breath, are merely one of many aspects of <u>this</u> ocurring at each moment.

The first step, then, in recognising the illusory nature of the mind's activity, is to establish a detached awareness which accords the same degree of recognition to external and internal stimuli. Whatever thoughts, ideas or disturbing passions arise are neither to be inhibited nor encouraged. If you simply serenely witness events, both inner and outer, without interference *and* sustain this practice for a minimum of a week, you will come to realise the illusory nature of inner activities.

As this meditation unfolds, you will find yourself utilising a technique you mastered as you strove to attain the first, or psychological, stage of enlightenment. At that stage in your meditation, you learned to monitor your awareness as it pivoted between your breathing and the endlessly absorbing streams of thought. In this meditation, you will learn to witness your awareness as it pivots between one-pointed focusing on the chosen stimulus, and one-pointed focusing on the endless process of the rising and falling away of thoughts.

As you witness the thoughts arising, without interference or any form of control, keeping your awareness as much as you are able on the chosen stimulus, the infinite relativity of all experience will gradually become clear to you. Every thought derives meaning and significance from the inner context, the underlying framework of assumptions, needs and desires, prejudices etc., in which it arises. As a result of your yogic training in these advanced Implicate Technology meditative practices, your mind will be able to move freely and spontaneously from context to context.

This ability of the spiritually developed mind to hop from context to context points to the illusory nature of the thought process. Any experience takes its meaning from the context in which it is understood. As your mind context-hops, so the significance, meaning and value attached to each experience undergoes change.

The yogically trained mind is able to understand and experience endlessly expanding horizons of meaning and significance. Every thought can be experienced as limited and conditioned by the process of the mind hopping to a wider, more all-embracing, context. There is literally no end to the contexts in which experience can be understood.

Infinitely, endlessly on and on, meaning and significance arise and fall away. The understanding you possess through thought at any moment is relative to the conditions implicit in the moment. Every thought occurs within infinitely fluctuating sets of conditions.

The fulness and richness of such experience points directly to its inherent emptiness and illusoriness. Your advanced meditation practice has only helped you to realise the infinite relativity of all conditioned experience. To attain enlightenment, you need direct intuitive experience of the absolute.

All relative experience is illusory, through being subject to change. All searching for the meaning and significance of life through utilising thought leads only to discovering yet another context to understand. To be absorbed in the infinite range of phenomenal experience is to be enmeshed in the illusion concealing the absolute, which is immanent in all relative experience.

☆ ☆ ☆ ☆

How is the relative, and so illusory, nature of conditioned experience to be transcended?

How are you to break free of the illusion of relative experience? How are you going to experience the absolute? How are you to break through and transcend the conditioned thought processes of your mind?

Begin by realising that you have arrived at the boundary of thought, you have reached the limits of what is thinkable and conceivable. Begin by realising that it is not possible to ascertain the true and absolute nature of everyday experience by thought. Reality can only be known by the clear, simple and direct experience of the transcendentally awakened and trained mind.

Having awoken to the transcendental nature of reality, the mind accepts what occurs, with simple directness. What occurs is accepted as it happens, because it is intuitively known and experienced as the conditioned form of mind in its absolute nature. Life is, as it spontaneously, harmoniously and inconceivably evolves across all of time towards the enlightenment of all of reality.

Be clear: even after you have attained the final stage of enlightenment, you will still be subject to the constraints of conditioned existence, you will still experience thoughts and emotions. The focus of awareness of an enlightened person can descend deep into conditioned existence. Suffering in his final agony, Jesus experienced a transient moment of desolation and despair, crying out: 'My God, my God, why hast thou forsaken me?'.

Thoughts cannot embrace the whole of reality. Mind in its transcendental state cannot be grasped or understood by thought. A mind operating at the transcendental level witnesses, embraces and goes beyond, first the individual thought process, and then, as the meditations unfold, all of conditioned existence.

Mind in its transcendental form is a still, thought-free awareness, which witnesses and intuitively understands thoughts as activities conditioning and constraining the direct intuitive experiencing of reality. Thoughts are understood and experienced as potent and attractive within the terms of reference of 'I'-based consciousness, the ultimately illusory, individual self. When the awareness is located in the transcendental state, one's own thoughts are observed with detachment, as spontaneous natural occurrences, like wind, snow or thunderstorms.

4.3 The realising of that.

You have transcended the illusion of separate individuality. You have awoken the mind's inherent capacity to experience the transcendental nature of reality. The remaining meditations in this chapter will teach you how to analyse this from the viewpoint of that, until you realise that this is that and only that.

Firstly, utilising your newly awakened transcendental powers of observation, you will meditate on the nature of time. When that is successfully completed, you will analyse, in meditation, the nature of mind and matter. Finally, you will discover through meditation that all things are products of mind in its unconditioned, universal, all-embracing form.

Once again, be in no hurry to advance through the meditations. Proceed in a spontaneous, relaxed manner. Meditate on each **bold** statement for a minimum of one day, and take as long as you need — there is no maximum.

If you have been meditating as instructed, you will now be able to explore the nature of reality with the direct intuitive awareness of mind in its transcendental state. You will begin by exploring the transcendental structure of your mind. As you come to understand the workings of mind through direct intuitive experience, you will, spontaneously and simultaneously, explore the true nature of <u>this</u>.

Every aspect of <u>this</u> is a construction of <u>that</u>, mind in its absolute and uncreated form, limited by the prevailing conditions. Your true nature transcends time, space, karma and all other conditions. Through exploring <u>this</u> from the viewpoint of <u>that</u>, you will overcome the ignorance obscuring direct experience of <u>that</u>.

In reality, every aspect of <u>this</u> is an illusorily objective component of the conditioned thought process of <u>that</u>. This means that these teachings, this book, your mind and body, the chair you sit on, the events of your life and all else, have their roots in <u>that</u>. You are now set on the path to transcending the illusion concealing from you that <u>this</u> is <u>that</u>.

When the dream is broken and you are conscious again of your true nature, <u>this</u> will still unfold as before. Your life will continue on its course; <u>this</u> does not vanish when the illusion is broken. If you have any doubts about the relative reality of <u>this</u>, try sticking a pin gently into your flesh – the resulting unpleasant sensation should convince you that <u>this</u> is a continuous process, lasting for the duration of time.

Despite the continuing everyday reality of your life and eventual death, you will gradually realise the illusorily objective nature of <u>this</u>. These meditations will cleanse your mind of its conditioned perceptions. Once you experience mind in its unconditioned state (or when you experience re-union with God, if you are inclined to religion), you will understand that <u>this</u> is illusory when experienced from the relative and objective perspective of mind in its unenlightened form, and that <u>this</u> is real when experienced from the absolute and subjective perspective of mind in its enlightened form.

As you proceed with the remaining meditations in this book, you must utilise simultaneously one-pointed awareness and the mind's inherent stillness, which transcends and embraces the thought process. That is to say, on the active level you will one-pointedly meditate on the given object, while simultaneously you will witness the one-pointed thought process with transcendent clarity. Intuition will supply understanding of the meditation, simultaneously expressed as a thought and as a direct transcendent experience of reality.

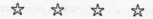

4.3.1 What is the nature of the present moment?

The preliminary Implicate Technology meditation on the nature of time is taught in chapter 5 of *Beyond the personality: the beginner's guide to enlightenment*. That meditation was designed to stabilise the awareness of a psychologically enlightened person in the understanding that reality occurs now, and only now. Be sure you understand that earlier meditation before starting on the meditation in this section.

One last word of advice before you begin the meditation: you are now in a mature phase of meditation. The heat of mental activity, creating the obscuring condensation on the window of perception, is diminishing along with the obscuring condensation. Remain calm as you begin to understand and experience clearly the nature of reality.

Do not fear as you intuitively experience the boundaries of space and time, life and death, crumble away. All that you will experience is the wonder and truth of your own nature. Nothing can happen to you that you are unable to deal with.

The past thought is no longer in existence. To the transcendentally awakened mind, enquiry into the nature of time and enquiry into the nature of existence are inseparable. This is because to exist is to be conditioned by time. Mind in its original and eternal state, that, transcends and embraces existence.

The structure and functioning of mind in its unenlightened state is a conditioned and limited form of mind in its natural and enlightened state. The processes of the conditioned mind are a faint and limited echo of mind in its serene and unconditioned state. By meditating one-pointedly on the nature of the mind's processes whilst simultaneously witnessing the meditation with the transcendentally awakened mind, direct intuitive experience of the nature of reality will unfold.

Only the present moment is in existence. Your previous thoughts have had their moments of existence and now no longer exist, except in memory. In the same way, the past thoughts of that, the previous configurations of the ten conditions which we experience as this, are no longer in existence.

The future thought, being not yet born, has not come into existence. The integrated, unified and purposefully evolving thought process of that unfolds conditioned existence, now. What will be is inherent in what is. The potential of this is realised as this is developed, by the thought process of <u>that</u>, towards conscious re-integration with <u>that</u>.

The present thought unfolds spontaneously and uncontrollably.

The meditative exercises in chapter 3 of this book taught you that it is impossible to stop or control the thought process, except for limited periods. The aim of this Western meditative system is to achieve detachment from the attractions and distractions of the thought process. As you are discovering day by day, the yogically trained mind witnesses with serene detachment the spontaneous coming in to existence of each thought.

You are now able serenely to witness a thought on one level of your being and at the same time spontaneously experience it on another level. In the same way, <u>that</u> witnesses <u>this</u> with clarity wisdom and delight in what is, and <u>that</u> experiences <u>this</u> simultaneously from your viewpoint, and her viewpoint, and his viewpoint, and my viewpoint. <u>This</u> evolves moment by moment, thought by thought, spontaneously and uncontrollably, according to the inherent implicate laws of conditioned existence.

Be clear: nothing exists independently of mind in its unconditioned state. No part of <u>this</u> exists independently from any other part. All of <u>this</u> has no existence in and of itself; it is <u>that</u> alone which gives <u>this</u> existence.

In chapter 5 of the first book in this Implicate Technology meditative system, you learned that to split time into past, present and future is unreal – they are each contained in the present moment. The meditation in this section teaches you that the present moment alone exists: moment by moment, <u>this</u> comes into existence and evolves through time. When you understand this intuitively, then you are ready to realise the illusory nature of birth, death and time.

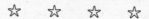

In what way are birth, death and time illusory?

Up to this point of beginning the meditation on the non-reality of birth, death and time, you have lived your life like a prisoner cast into a dark cell. The stark reality of your life is that you have spent your time stumbling about in the gloom, getting by as best you could. In the ignorance and obscuring darkness of mind in its unenlightened state, you have been incapable of understanding the true nature of the experiences conveyed to you by your five senses.

Yet, in your darkness, ignorance and isolation, you have progressed with unwavering determination in your daily practice of meditation. This practice has served to develop and strengthen your sixth sense, your inherent powers of intuitive insight into the nature of reality. You do not yet realise it, but the key has already been turned in the cell door; you have awakened the transcendent aspect of mind and you are free to leave the cell of conditioned existence.

Once out of the cell, you will have to travel the corridors of the prison until you reach the exit. You must be careful as you travel towards enlightenment and freedom; karma is still functioning to test your detachment from, and serenity in the face of, life's experiences.

You have earned the right to leave behind your darkness and ignorance. These teachings will guide you out of the confining prison of ignorance of reality. Come, gather your determination and courage: as you travel along the corridors of space and time, mind and matter, life and death, you will discover that they exist only in the materialised and illusorily objective thought process of <u>that</u>, and being <u>that</u> in your true nature you transcend all of <u>this</u>.

Firstly, become aware of your limitations. You have only travelled just over half way along the path to the final stage of enlightenment. Although you will soon be capable of intuitively grasping the nature of the illusion, it will only be transcended when you attain the final stage of enlightenment.

Be clear: at no time will your daily life dissolve away to reveal the reality beyond time and space. Any such experiences are simply an extension of the illusion, a function of the mind's illusory and conditioned activities. Your daily life is unreal and illusory when experienced from the unenlightened viewpoint, and the real expression of the perfection of <u>that</u> when experienced from the enlightened viewpoint.

The illusion, obscuring true and direct intuitive experience of the nature of reality, lies in the mistaken interpretation of sensual experience which leads you to think, 'I live, I age and one day I will die'. The reality is that what ages and dies is the body. The reality is that it is not 'I' who lives, but <u>that</u> which lives us.

70

Only that, which transcends, embraces and is conditioned existence is not subject to the conditions of time and space. With your newly awakened capacity to witness this with the silent, serene and transcendental awareness of that, meditate on the true nature of time. Be still, witness the one-pointed meditation process and know the truth through direct intuitive experience.

From the viewpoint of the individual, birth, ageing, suffering and death are inevitable. From the transcendental viewpoint of that, individuality is only relatively real, and so, too, are birth, ageing, suffering and death. **That, in its absolute nature, is unborn and not subject to birth, ageing, suffering and death.**

Time holds sway over the thought process of that. That is to say, your body and your individuality, being conditioned constructs of that, are subject to time, life and death. The reality is that in your own nature you are that, and only that.

Just as you are witnessing your one-pointed meditation with a serene awareness transcending thought, so that witnesses this. The gap between your mind's conditioned activity and the serenity of transcendental awareness is the pulse, the duration, of one thought. **This comes into and goes out of existence thought by thought.**

The gap between existence conditioned by time and unconditioned awareness transcending time is the pulse of one thought. The measure of the gap between the eternal incarnate cycle of birth and death, and being transcending incarnation, is the duration of one thought. **Duration through time is immersion in, and attachment to, the thought process of that.**

4.3.2 In what way do mind and matter spring from a single source?

Are mind and matter separate?

Viewed from the narrow, limited and relatively illusory standpoint of mind in its individual and unenlightened form, there is a clear distinction between mind and matter. Viewed from the all-embracing and absolutely subjective standpoint of mind in its enlightened supra-individual form, both the individual mind and matter are intuitively known as illusorily separated and objectified products of that, the one universal mind which alone is. From the religious point of view, both mind and matter find a common source in God.

The transcending of the illusion that mind and matter are separate is achieved by the act of witnessing one-pointed meditation on the question printed above in **bold**. Take as long as you need to meditate on the question above. When your intuition enables you to understand the general principle involved, then move on to the more detailed one-pointed meditations which follow.

Deluded and confused by the apparent sensuous reality of this, mind in its unenlightened form has forgotten its origin and true nature. Mind has become unconscious of the reality that this is merely the product of its own thought process. The true goal is realisation of mind in its original state, transcending its thought products.

What is the nature of matter?

All material substance is an objectified product of mind in its unconditioned form. The individual mind, the unique point of view on this, is a thought product with only relative reality. From the relatively real (and equally so, the relatively illusory) perspective of individual perception, matter is both tangible and separate from mind. From the absolute, universal and real perspective of that, both matter and the individual mind which experiences this are simply conditioned thought products manifesting and unfolding simultaneously.

All of this is the unity, harmony and endless perfection of that made manifest. The mind, on becoming enlightened, accepts and understands the inherent harmony, wonder and perfection of this. Not having realised its true source and being in that, the unenlightened mind experiences this across all of time as endless birth, ageing, suffering and death. That is to say, the unenlightened mind is eternally immersed in the illusion of material reality.

How can the shape, colour and texture of objects be a product of mind?

Using the five senses as a guide, the shape, colour and texture of objects is clearly 'out there', an inherent property of all objects. Using the sixth sense as a guide, properly developed under a coherent and structured system of meditation, the relationship between the object perceived, the person perceiving and the act of perception is understood

72

in a direct, intuitive way. Meditation-enhanced intuition informs the meditator that both the mind which perceives sensuous objects and the objects themselves are illusorily separate thought products of the one and only mind.

The act of perception is inseparable from the perceiver and that which is perceived. From the absolute perspective of the enlightened mind, all experience of sensuous reality – the everyday world we live in – is the product of projected concepts of the one mind. **The experiencer, the experienced and the act of experiencing are all relative concepts of the one, universal, all-embracing mind**.

All ephemeral things, this in its entirety, are produced, experienced and witnessed by mind in its unconditioned form. Both this and the thought in your head are products of that. There is a profound identity between a thought and this.

You have learnt from practice of the advanced meditations that thoughts arise spontaneously and uncontrollably, as a response to the stimuli of conditioned existence. Thoughts come into and go out of existence with immeasurable suddenness. Every thought is replaced by another, endlessly.

All of this is a thought of that. This comes into and goes out of existence with the rapidity and spontaneity of thought. This is so, because that thinks it to be so.

From the absolute viewpoint of mind in its enlightened state, this is witnessed in the same way as you have been learning to witness your own thought process. To travel along the path towards the final stage of enlightenment, act spontaneously, without interfering and with unwavering acceptance. To become enlightened, Live and Act.

How does ignorance of the true nature of this come about?

Mind in its unenlightened state is deluded and confused by the apparent sensuous reality of this. Enlightenment clears away all errors and confusions about the nature of sensuous reality. You cannot know the world aright until you clear your mind of ignorance of the nature of reality.

Through incarnation after incarnation, as mind in its individual form experiences this, it becomes seduced by desire for more experience. Across immeasurable time, the individual mind forgets its real and enduring relation to that and comes to know only the limited and illusory experience of individual separateness. Mind only forgets, or

73

becomes unconscious of, the truth that this is that: knowledge of the true nature of reality is always dormant in the mind, needing only meditative practices to re-awaken perception of the truth.

This current life is just one part of your long, long journey across the endless sea of this, the endless ocean of sensuous reality. The illusory and unreal goal is desire for the fruits of this – love, fame, wealth, possessions, power, success, health and all other sensuous experiences. The real goal of all lives is the realisation of mind in its true nature, not immersion in its thought products.

All suffering, all uncertainty, all confusion is caused by ignorance of your own mind and nature. All sorrow can be transcended by realising and remaining in mind in its natural state. All fully developed spiritual paths make direct experience of the truth of reality accessible to anyone who seeks in a harmonious, natural and humble way.

4.3.3 In what way are all the many separate aspects of this really that?

Is this a single thing?

When witnessed with a mind which has been awakened transcendentally, this is perceived in its true nature as a vast, organic, infinitely cross-connected living unity. All thinking minds, all things with life, all inanimate matter, are thought products of the one all-embracing mind. All processes, both natural and devised by humanity, all natural laws, both explicate and implicate, all moral, judicial and social systems are thought by that, and so come into existence.

That witnesses this without interference or desire. Mind in its unenlightened form experiences this within the terms of the karmically reactive system. Only with the dawning of enlightenment does the mind become freed from the thrall of karma.

Or is this a plural thing?

Things are seen, experienced and understood as plural and separate by the thinking mind. Inherently based on the 'I'-thought, thinking creates an illusory experience of fundamental separateness, apartness and loneliness. The transcendentally awakened mind, clear, serene and filled with an awareness transcending thought, becomes conscious of the true, inherently unified nature of reality.

How can <u>this</u> be a single thing when it is manifestly innumerable separate things?

<u>That</u> is immanent in every component part and process of <u>this</u>. Every person is a unique focus of experience of <u>this</u>, capable of becoming conscious of the truth of reality, that <u>this</u> is <u>that</u>. Every living thing and every inanimate object is as much an integral part of <u>this</u> as you or I.

How can <u>this</u> be separate things, since in its true nature each thing is <u>that</u>?

<u>This</u> is illusory when experienced from the relative, separate and individual point of view; <u>this</u> is real when experienced from the absolute, integrated and transcendental point of view. The illusion that people and things are separate and real in themselves is a product of ignorance. The illusion that <u>this</u> is real in itself has been broken through sustained, committed daily practice of advanced meditation – transcendentally aware, you see only that <u>this</u> is <u>that</u>.

4.4 The realising of reality

The third stage of enlightenment has now been realised. It is characterised by the intuitive experience of seeing and experiencing all things as <u>that</u>. The illusion that things exist independently, in themselves, is broken forever.

Rest now, before resuming your journey. The goal is so close now – if you are seeking God, you will soon be re-united; if you are seeking the unconditioned state, you will soon realise it. Rest for a while, and witness <u>this</u>, with effortless spontaneity, in its true nature as <u>that</u>.

This is that

The contents and experiences of a dream are real to the dreaming mind. On awakening, everyday reality is known and experienced on its own terms. There is nothing else but <u>that</u> to see, know or experience.

The activities of dreams are <u>that</u>.

Being woken by the alarm, or a lover's touch, is <u>that</u>.

Brushing your teeth, washing your face and emptying your bowels is <u>that</u>.

Bodily pleasures, discomforts and pains are <u>that</u>, configured by karma to direct your awareness.

Dressing, eating and embarking on the day's activities are <u>that</u>.

There is no such thing as inactivity for the unenlightened person – only the mind capable of witnessing <u>this</u> as <u>that</u> can be truly still.

The events of the day, your interaction with people, places and things is the unfolding of <u>that</u>.

Desire for gratification of the senses is <u>that</u>.

Lack of desire for gratification of the senses is <u>that</u>.

The experience of sensual satisfaction is <u>that</u>.

The absence of sensual fulfilment is <u>that</u>.

The calm acceptance of what you receive as being what you get is <u>that</u>.

Intense, committed and impersonal effort to change what is unjust is <u>that</u>.

The endless and futile pursuit of illusory and transient goals, characteristic of the unenlightened mind, is <u>that</u>.

All of <u>this</u> is <u>that</u>

5 *The path to the final stage of enlightenment*

<u>That</u> manifests itself as <u>this</u>. The illusorily separate components of <u>this</u> have existed in ignorance of their true nature, lifetime after lifetime, remaining attracted and deluded by desire for experience of <u>this</u>. Purged at last of ignorance of the nature of reality, the transcendentally awakened mind becomes fully conscious of the inherent and absolute unity of <u>this</u> and <u>that</u>, through the process of transcendental yoga.

What is the process of attaining the final and absolute stage of enlightenment?

The transcendentally awakened mind witnesses <u>this</u> with a serene, tranquil clarity. The analysis of the nature of reality is completed by practice of the transcendental yoga taught in this chapter. Step by step you will learn, from direct intuitive experience, that <u>this</u> and <u>that</u> are now, have always been and will always be, inseparable.

In reaching this stage in your meditations, you have been supported by the profound intuitive conviction that reality is an inherent unity. Step by step, in chapter 4, you came to understand the underlying unity of all things. Now, in chapter 5, you will learn to experience this unity directly.

With the intuitive certainty of the transcendentally awakened mind, you now have the unshakeable conviction that there is a final stage of enlightenment. Know as a certainty that, with a last sustained effort, you will experience directly, in and for yourself, the final and absolute nature of reality. The process of enlightenment is now so advanced that it has become virtually inexorable; it is now only a matter of time and practice, provided you maintain unwavering determination to reach the end of your journey.

Firstly, you will recognise through direct intuitive experience that this is entirely a mental product of that. You will recognise that the world is the materialised and illusorily externalised thought process of the one mind, which alone is. You will learn simultaneously to participate in and transcend this thought process – that is to say, you will learn to participate in, and simultaneously transcend, conditioned existence.

Secondly, you will recognise that there is no difference at all between this and that, except ignorance of the nature of reality. You will understand through experience that this and that are different states of the one, inherent unity. Witnessing this from the real and absolute viewpoint of that, or experiencing this from the relative and illusory individual viewpoint, are simply two sides of the same coin.

Thirdly, you will experience all things as one. This and that are inseparable. 'You' and 'I' and everything else will be known and experienced in their real and absolute nature as an inseparable, all-embracing and infinitely harmonious unity.

Finally, according to your nature, you will come to the end of your journey. If you are of a religious and devotional inclination, you will become at one with God. If you are of a secular and analytical inclination, you will realise the unconditioned state.

Regardless of whether you are secular or religious by nature, the potential for good, afforded by your journey and your effort, will have been significantly wasted if you regard enlightenment as a prize you have attained for your own benefit. The fully conscious component of reality, the fully enlightened person, is an empty vehicle driven by an unseen hand, a selfless tool devoid of individual volition and dedicated to the enlightenment of all others. At one with reality, motivated by infinite compassion for the suffering of others, act according to your intuition to heal, to help and to enlighten.

☆　　☆　　☆　　☆

How do you set about recognising that this is entirely a mental product of that?

It can happen that you dream deeply, with great involvement and attachment to the contents of your dream. On awakening, your mind can be confused – the dream can seem more real and more desirable than your ordinary, everyday life. Sometimes it is with a struggle that you shake off the effects of such a dream; sometimes you have to work hard to clear your mind of the lingering effects of an attractive illusion.

That situation is exactly the one you find yourself in at this stage in your meditation. You have awoken from the dream which obscured the nature of reality from you. You no longer live, eat, breathe and think in ignorance – you know with intuitive certainty that <u>this</u> is <u>that</u>.

Now you must undertake the final meditative practices which cleanse your mind of lingering confusion about the nature of reality. Just as the 'I' which experiences reality in the dream is a product of your dreaming mind, so, too, is your individual sense of 'I', your specific and unique human individuality, a product of <u>that</u> in its unenlightened or dreaming state. Whatever your dreaming mind experiences is simply a product of your own thought process. Similarly, whatever 'I' experience in ordinary, everyday life, of self, others or things, is simply part of the thought process of <u>that</u>.

To experience that <u>this</u> is <u>that</u>, you need do nothing. The relaxed, transcendentally awakened mind naturally and effortlessly understands and experiences all external and internal phenomena as the product of the one, universal, all-embracing mind. Alternatively, and equally validly, the religiously inclined, transcendentally awakened mind naturally and effortlessly experiences all of <u>this</u> as subject to the will of, and immersed in the love of, God.

From a religious or a secular point of view, the relaxed transcendent witnessing of <u>this</u> makes manifest the underlying characteristic of conditioned existence. From the transcendent viewpoint of <u>that</u>, all of conditioned existence is suffused with infinite love. Out of that all-embracing, unstinting, all-giving love arises endless compassion for the suffering of the unenlightened.

Understand, experience and witness now the ecstatic love which is the union of <u>this</u> and <u>that</u>. The whole of reality, experienced as an inexpressible unity, is the eternally ecstatic interaction of stillness and movement. Like two lovers absorbed in sexual delight, the separate parts find fulfillment in unity.

Through realisation of the eternal unity of movement and stillness, love for all of <u>this</u> is born. Through action born of profound meditation, universal love is expressed. From deepest samadhi springs selfless intuitive action to heal, to help and to enlighten.

The way of action, the way of knowledge of reality and the way of love are inextricably interwoven. Express your love for <u>this</u> through intuitive action, devoid of individual volition. Love flows from understanding and experiencing the inseparableness, the inherent unity, of conditioned existence.

Throughout your life, <u>Live</u> and <u>Act</u>.

☆　　☆　　☆　　☆

How do you set about identifying <u>this</u> as <u>that</u>?

Up to this point in your meditations, you have viewed <u>this</u> from a relative perspective, located and rooted in <u>this</u>. Even with the awakening of the transcendent aspects of mind, you have still experienced conditioned existence within the restraining constructs of the ten conditions. Know as a certainty that for the rest of your life you will continue to experience <u>this</u> from a relative viewpoint – after all, like everyone else, you are only an ordinary mortal person.

Know also as a certainty that, as a result of successful completion of this meditation, your perspective on <u>this</u> will in addition simultaneously reveal the absolute nature of <u>this</u>. Practice of this meditation marks the shift in your consciousness from abiding only in <u>this</u>, to living in <u>this</u> while knowing and experiencing it as <u>that</u>. Know as a certainty that you will experience <u>this</u> from the absolute viewpoint of <u>that</u> – like everyone else, you are an incarnation of the universal, all-embracing mind; in religious terms, we are all children of the one God.

All of <u>this</u>, every part and aspect of the eternal process, arises, occurs and ceases to exist as the thought process of <u>that</u> unfolds. All of <u>this</u>, in its implicate and explicate aspects, has reality only through the workings of the thought process of <u>that</u>. From the absolute perspective of <u>that</u>, <u>this</u> is known and experienced in its true nature; once re-union with God has been attained, the world is known as it is.

Understood with the transcendent serenity of mind in its unconditioned state, <u>this</u> in its totality is known as the manifest form of <u>that</u>. <u>That</u> expresses itself, in its fulness, as <u>this</u>. <u>That</u> is formless, yet gives shape, meaning and purpose to <u>this</u>.

80

This and that are intertwined, indissolubly and eternally.
Conditioned existence cannot be understood in its true nature without experiencing it with the mind in its unconditioned state. God and the world are ever one, united in a loving embrace.

This and that are of one nature, two sides of the same coin.
That thinks this, manifests this and experiences this, whilst simultaneously transcendentally witnessing the whole process. The thinker and the thought are one and the same.

This is that, subject to the constraints of the ten conditions.
The joys and horrors of this are the result of the corrective reaction of karma to individual and collective thoughts and actions. Karma shapes the lives and minds of countless components of this across space and time, evolving this as a whole towards recollection of its original nature as that.

As a result of meditating one-pointedly on these teachings with a transcendentally awakened mind, the true nature of this becomes clear to you. As you have been taught throughout this Implicate Technology teaching of the clear setting face to face with reality, this is the manifest form of that. Understood in its true nature, this is that. In your true nature, transcending outer form and difference, you, everybody and everything else are that.

Before completing your journey to enlightenment, pause to survey this from the perspective of that. That witnesses this with a profound and serene detachment. Follow the meditations to explore the three-fold nature of transcendental witnessing.

This three-fold nature is the expression of the highest, purest and simplest state of consciousness within conditioned existence. To the monotheist, it is the three-fold nature of God; to the Hindu, it is Sat-Chit-Ananda – Being, Consciousness and Bliss; to the Buddhist, it is the first reflex in conditioned existence of mind in its unconditioned state. Within the framework of Implicate Technology, it is the three-fold nature of transcendental witnessing.

By this penultimate meditation, you are learning the three-fold nature of your own experience in its purest of conditioned forms. The transcendentally aware mind witnesses this, knowing and experiencing it as that, with clarity, wisdom and delight. Live your ordinary, everyday life knowing the ecstatic bliss of transcendental witnessing, without the

81

need to express your inner experience through outer sign.

The person who has realised these highest teachings of Implicate Technology, through direct intuitive experience, has no need to shout aloud the good news. Regardless of outer form, the life of a fully enlightened person is dedicated, with unremitting inner perseverance, to helping all others to attain enlightenment. The primary means of achieving this is action, not words.

The enlightened person loves <u>this</u> with a simple, direct and entirely spontaneous humility. You now exist to serve others by helping them along the path to enlightenment. Express your love and compassion for <u>this</u> through direct intuitive <u>Action</u>.

The first reflex of <u>that</u>, in conditioned form, is transcendental consciousness witnessing <u>this</u> with clarity, wisdom and delight. Witnessing what is, the fully realised transcendent mind is only one meditative step from realising mind in its unconditioned state. It is a matter of personal preference which of these two ultimate realisations you choose as your final goal.

For some, particularly those who are religiously inclined, realisation of mind in its purest conditioned form of transcendental witness is experienced as re-unification with God. For others, particularly those who experience the spiritual path as a search to understand the nature of reality rather than as a search for re-union with God, the goal is not reached until mind in its unconditioned state is realised. Both realisations are the final and absolute stage of enlightenment, experienced and expressed from different viewpoints.

<u>That</u> is clarity

<u>That</u>, in its purest conditioned form as transcendent witness of <u>this</u>, is an awareness of utter clarity. <u>That</u> is an experience of clarity, untainted and unblemished by any form of desire. <u>That</u> witnesses, but does not participate in, desires of any nature for any object, whether it be tangible or intangible.

<u>That</u> simultaneously transcends and witnesses the ten conditions structuring the development of its manifest thought process. <u>That</u> is untouched by fear or desire, untouched by any weakness or limitation. <u>That</u> simply is awareness of what is, untainted by any form of desire.

82

That is wisdom

In its first reflex as transcendent witness of this, that is an awareness of pure, clear wisdom. That is aware of the necessity, form and purpose of the ten conditions. That witnesses this clearly, knowing the true meaning of what is experienced.

The wisdom of that is an awareness of this in the context of the movement of this towards re-union with that. That is the consciousness that this unfolds in an endless, unified and harmonious movement towards recollecting that it is that. That is the wisdom to witness this, knowing the nature and purpose of what is.

That is delight

Untainted by desire, aware of the nature and purpose of what is, that witnesses this with delight. The horror, the pain and the suffering of this, the joy, the hope and the happiness of this, are all known in their true nature. Understanding the true, final and absolute nature of everyday life, that witnesses with delight the unfolding of this.

All experience is only real relative to the one who experiences. When sought in a yogically disciplined manner, the individual, the one who experiences separateness, cannot be found. In the final analysis of the mind enlightened through practice of yoga, all experience is unreal – it is known to be of the nature of a passing dream.

All suffering is only real relative to the one who experiences. Mind in its fully realised transcendent state of unsullied witness knows intuitively the inherent unreality of what is experienced as suffering. That delights in the true nature of what is.

Witnessing this with clarity wisdom and delight, the transcendentally awakened mind comes at last to experience the inherent unity of all things.

What is the inherent unity of all things?

Meditate on the nature of an ordinary event. Two people meet, sit down to talk and eat, embrace briefly and leave. What is the reality of this occurrence?

To the unenlightened person, this situation is unclear, requiring much more background before its significance can be understood. Who are these people? What is their purpose in meeting? Is it by design or by chance? What is their relationship? Is their purpose business or pleasure, lawful or clandestine? The questions can go on indefinitely – it is a truism of mind in its unenlightened form that you can never really know another person.

Mind in its unenlightened state experiences only separateness and illusion. Hampered by the basic inability to understand the true nature of ordinary experience, the unenlightened person compounds the difficulties by constructing a view of reality based on individual experience. That is to say, ignorant of what is really happening at any given moment, the unenlightened person relies on opinions – which often masquerade as objective facts – to understand reality.

Opinions are the curse of the unenlightened. Opinions are a dead-weight dragging the unenlightened deeper and deeper into the illusion of separate and independent existence. The enlightened person has no inherent need of opinions.

To the enlightened person, this ordinary situation is quite clear, requiring no more background before its significance can be understood. In reality, the situation is exactly as it is. Two people meet, sit down to talk and eat, embrace briefly and leave.

If the enlightened mind needs to know any background information, that knowledge arises effortlessly. If any action is required, that action takes place spontaneously and effortlessly. From the inner point of view of enlightened experience, everything occurs spontaneously and effortlessly.

Mind in its enlightened state experiences with clarity and unity. All things are known in their true form as being merely objective mani-festations of that. The only true difference between the unenlightened and the enlightened person is that the former is ignorant of the true nature of reality and the latter is not.

The enlightened person deals only with what is, as it occurs. Knowing the evolutionary nature of karma, accepting and understanding the events of life as the workings of karma, the enlightened person – established in clarity – sees, experiences and knows only that. Clear, wise and filled with delight, the transcendentally realised mind knows conditioned existence in its true nature as all-embracing mind.

Able to function in the everyday world – to love, to work, to build and to heal – the enlightened person sees no real differences, no true separation. Knowing your own mind is <u>that</u>, you walk in the world seeing others and the world as <u>that</u>. Motivated by unbounded compassion for the world's ignorance and suffering, your life is dedicated to helping others onto and along the path.

☆ ☆ ☆ ☆

What is the meditation to effect realisation of the inherent unity of <u>this</u> and <u>that</u>?

Everything is in its place. On both the individual and the transcendental levels, your mind has been disciplined and prepared. You are ready to understand through direct intuitive experience the inherent unity of conditioned existence and immanent, transcendent mind.

In your progress along the path, you will have already glimpsed the final stage of enlightenment in brief flashes. You will have briefly and intermittently experienced a stillness and peace transcending and embracing all else. Practice of this meditation will stabilise your consciousness in the state of enduring freedom termed the final stage of enlightenment.

With mind in its transcendentally awakened and still state, witness <u>this</u>, intuitively experiencing and accepting it as <u>that</u>. Simultaneously meditate one-pointedly, repeating over and over in your mind: everything is as it should be. Continue with your ordinary life without interruption, analysis or interference.

This one-pointed meditation transmutes any lingering uncertainties into the experience of transcendent unity. All of <u>this</u> is intuitively known in its true form as the inherently unified manifestation of <u>that</u>. All separateness and individuality is directly known as an illusion, born of ignorance and masking the true nature of reality.

This ultimate experience of serenity and peace, transcending all conditions, is impossible to convey in words. It is likened to a vast ocean, utterly still. 'It is indescribable by use of speech, and is not an object of the mind.' [1]

---

[1]   Evans-Wentz W. Y.; *Tibetan Yoga and Secret Doctrines*; Oxford, Oxford University Press, 1967, page 150.

To the religiously inclined, enlightenment is experienced as unity with God. Re-united in the love of God, the truth about the world is known and experienced directly. The terrible and illusory cycle of life and death is transcended in direct experience of the world as divine.

To the secular mind, enlightenment is experienced as a state of unconditioned awareness. Conditioned existence is witnessed, experienced and participated in with clarity, wisdom and delight, from a perspective of absolute subjectivity, transcending karma, space and time and all the other conditions. <u>This</u> is known with intuitive directness as illusory, being only relatively real and lacking in the absolute reality inherent in <u>that</u>.

Now that the far journey has ended, survey and secure what you have won.

The far journey to understand and experience the true nature of reality is over. Begun long, long ago, the struggle to end your ignorance is finally and irrevocably over. You know who you are, and you know the true nature of what you experience during each moment.

In Implicate Technology teaching this is called the clear setting face to face with reality. Transcendentally still and clear, you experience reality as it is, directly and without ignorance or illusion. Reality is <u>that</u>, <u>this</u> is <u>that</u>, you are <u>that</u>.

That relative and illusory component of mind which comprises your individual mind has been transcended – so much so, that the purity of original mind is no longer tainted and corrupted by individual choice. Your whole psycho-physiological system has become a driverless vehicle, a tool for the use of <u>that</u>. Transcendentally serene and clear, your mind and body is, from the point of view of your inner experience, an empty shell devoid of volition.

Acting as a direct expression of <u>that</u>, you no longer have a propensity to act in such a way as to incur negative or positive karma. Your ordinary, everyday state of consciousness transcends the karmically reactive system. The lesson of reality has been learnt.

Although your mind may be free from the influence of karma, provided you maintain transcendental serenity, your body is not and cannot be free. Your body is a product of karma and that karma must be experienced. That is to say, your body must experience ageing, suffering and death according to its destiny.

In addition, you will be subject to the vast aggregations of individual karma, incurred across waves of incarnations, shaping cultural and global history. An enlightened person can be swept up in events every bit as much as an unenlightened person. Being enlightened does not exempt you from AIDS, terrorism, nuclear war, race war, economic deprivation or any other event of life.

Yet whatever may be the destiny of your body or your time, your mind has irrevocably won freedom. You may temporarily drift or fall from the state of absolute clarity, wisdom and delight, but you cannot lose what you have won. Any drift from direct experience of the absolute can only be temporary – Jesus's agony and doubt on the cross, 'My God, my God, why has thou forsaken me?', was only the momentary result of a transient set of conditions.

If you do slide back into the karmically reactive system, then karma will guide you back into the enlightened state of mind. You have no need any more to practise meditation daily. You are now capable of living in meditation, although occasionally you may need to meditate formally to regain inner serenity.

The experience of mind in its unconditioned state at first seems bland. It feels, at first, like an infinity of stillness devoid of qualities and interest. This is simply due to unfamiliarity with the unutterably inexhaustible source of all forms of experience.

As a result of the initial impression of blandness, you may be tempted to retrace your steps along the path – simply because there is more apparent richness of experience, and more familiarity, in the events of the past. Resist that temptation; learn to maintain your consciousness in this new state of mind, just as you did at the beginning of samadhi. Although demanding at first, it will rapidly become second nature to remain in the unconditioned state.

The key to maintaining the final stage of enlightenment is to keep the mind in its natural state. Steadfastly remain in the qualityless stillness, transcending all conditions and all forms of mental activity: such as memory, anticipation, analysis and all forms of emotion or thought. Simply experience that, mind in its natural and unconditioned state, knowing that such experience is inexpressible and incommunicable.

Witnessing this with clarity, wisdom and delight, know that you are no different from anybody else. Knowing the nature of the illusion that is objective reality, be guided by karma as you work to help others along the path. Live for the service and benefit of others, according to your intuition.

As you work to help others understand the true nature of their experience and their suffering, always direct them towards overcoming the limitations they place on their own minds. Crippled by some combination of selfishness, stupidity, lust, greed or fear, the unenlightened person unknowingly limits the possibility of a fulfilled life. Treat each person uniquely and respect their limitations and weaknesses.

Explain to others only what they are capable of understanding at the time of explanation. Your goal is always to help them take the next step along the path. There is no hurry – this, with its ignorance and suffering, will last for an infinite length of time.

Witnessing this with the unconditioned clarity of that, know that conditioned existence and its inherent suffering are both unreal. Ignorance gives suffering the illusion of reality. Yet this is no game or pretence, and until the last unenlightened person knows that from direct intuitive experience, the endless cycle of birth, ageing, suffering and death will continue.

Time, ignorance and suffering last infinitely long, yet have only relative reality. The process that is conditioned existence will continue to unfold for the duration of time, witnessed and experienced by the absolute and only mind which embraces and transcends mere existence. Now that you have attained enlightenment for your psychophysiological system's individual mind, your greatest contribution to the general good lies in helping others along the path towards release from suffering.

☆   ☆   ☆   ☆

What is effortless activity?

Serenely transcending the illusion that conditioned existence is an objective reality and witnessing this clearly in its true nature as the manifest form of unconditioned mind, the fully realised mind continues to live out the life of the body. Wholeheartedly embracing everyday life, the enlightened person loves, works, cares, contributes and offers service to others. No matter how much work the enlightened person appears to do, no matter how much effort a fully enlightened mind appears to expend, the inner experience of an enlightened mind is of effortless activity.

The enlightened experience is of desirelessness, of contentment and acceptance. What is done is done at the moment of action, as a direct expression of <u>that</u>, without desire or regard for the consequences. No personal gain is sought, because the personal, and the experience of gain and loss, are known in their illusory nature.

Expressed in religious terms, the enlightened person does only the will of God. Desiring nothing, exerting no effort of mind, God's will is enacted through the enlightened person. The fully realised mind places no barriers between the world and the expression of God's will.

Fully involved in everyday life – loving, laughing, crying, ageing, suffering and dying – the enlightened person experiences <u>this</u> with the body and the individual mind, and simultaneously witnesses <u>this</u> with the transcendentally realised mind. Everything is experienced as occurring without effort, even if the body and the individual mind are exhausted from working. Only the body, and the mind in its conditioned individual and separate form, work; mind in its fully realised state is ever serene and free.

In the final analysis, it is only desire which binds mind in its unenlightened state to conditioned existence. Freed from the bonds of desire, the enlightened person lives in the world and knows its inherent unreality. Enmeshed in desire, the unenlightened person lives in ignorance, mistaking the world itself for reality.

As an enlightened person, it is not given to you to make the rest of the world enlightened. You cannot take away the pain of existence for innumerable individuals. The world's suffering will continue for measureless time. But by offering your service, according to your nature, to those seeking enlightenment, you will be doing the maximum possible to alleviate the world's ignorance and consequent suffering.

<u>Live</u>, <u>Act</u> and serve others, according to your intuition.

6   The four formless absorptions

Embark upon the four formless absorptions, knowing with the unshakeable certainty of direct experience that <u>this</u> is <u>that</u>. Become aware of the principles of construction of conditioned existence whilst living your ordinary everyday life. Without the need for daily meditation, explore and know the manifest form of mind in its original, pure and unmanifest nature.

What are the four formless absorptions?

Conditioned existence is the manifest form of God. <u>This</u> is mind's original, formless and untainted nature locked in the relatively illusory and dream-like process of evolving back to conscious realisation of its original, formless and untainted nature. <u>This</u> in its entirety is the name of God, which no individual mind can encompass.

One by one, practice of these four absorptions peels away dependence on form, to reveal, to the enlightened understanding, direct intuitive experience of the formless and absolute nature of reality. Through increasingly subtle perceptions of the nature of the form and underlying structure of the process of conditioned existence, the true nature of the merely objective processes of reality becomes known. The reality of the apparently objective framework in which we live, the world of nature, is explored through these absorptions and traced to its formless roots in the absolute subjectivity of mind in its unconditioned form.

These absorptions are simply natural and spontaneous extensions and refinements of the fourth and final stage of enlightenment. It is as though, having scaled your way up a steep cliff, you arrive at the top to discover a vast plateau, and, instead of having to progress inch by inch, you can now explore huge areas with ease. These absorptions simply release knowledge of reality which has lain dormant in your mind; the plateau, the explorer and the act of exploration are, and have always been, an indivisible unity.

A characteristic of the fully realised mind is the experience of separateness and multiplicity as an illusion concealing the underlying unity of reality. The enlightened mind is primarily focused on the unity of reality; in religious terms, the enlightened mind is primarily focused on God. Such intense and simple concentration is the result of the sustained meditative practices mastered on the journey to enlightenment; except for brief periods of meditation to restore temporary disruptions of equanimity, you should have no further need of meditation.

To practise these absorptions, let your mind turn simply and naturally to the subject of each absorption. Allow your intuition to guide you as you explore the structure underpinning conditioned existence. Whatever knowledge comes to you in these absorptions, be clear: the manifest world of nature is simply an externalised and objectified aspect of the universal and all-embracing, original and formless mind of which you are a conscious and microscopic part.

Become absorbed in the base consisting of infinite space.

Witnessing the unfolding of conditioned existence with the unobscured clarity of the enlightened mind, you can transcend the relative and illusory perception of form. Every apparently separate person, place and thing is known to you in its true nature as a manifest product of the one and only mind in its unconditioned state. The ordinary everyday perception of the enlightened mind transcends mere appearances and intuitively apprehends the underlying unity.

With direct perception of the nature of reality comes spontaneous absorption in the flow of reality. The enlightened mind, aware of the karmic patterning which shapes and directs each moment, offers no resistance to the will of God. The futile conflict between individual desire and the flow of reality is resolved through unwavering acceptance of things as they are.

There are no choices for the enlightened mind to make. Knowing intuitively the actions to take, the enlightened person acts as karma determines. The enlightened life is lived in the effortless freedom of moving through the world while experiencing it as the manifest form of that.

91

The enlightened person pays no attention to apparent differences between self and others. All are known intuitively in their true nature as inherent equals, and all are taught according to their current level of consciousness. Underlying all appearance of difference is the one unified unconditioned mind; God alone is and all is God.

Leaving behind perceptions of form, resistance and difference, become aware of infinite space.

All activities, all experience, all things take place within the ever-unfolding context of the thought-process of the one universal mind, which forms, embraces and transcends conditioned existence. That, the Absolute Godhead, the Absolute Brahman, the Void, is outside of existence in its true and absolute nature. Only limited and conditioned things come into existence.

Existence is a conditioned and constrained construct of the one mind in its natural, original and unconditioned state. That devolves into conditioned form, as infinite extension through infinite space. The human mind, evolved by the far journey to the final and absolute stage of enlightenment into re-unification with that, becomes aware of the base comprising infinite space.

The infinite expanse of this is the conditioned form of that. Be still, absorbed in the base consisting of infinite space. Become aware of the unity pervading all of space and transcending all of time.

Become absorbed in the base consisting of infinite consciousness.

Leaving behind perceptions of infinite space, become aware of infinite consciousness. Infinitely extended throughout this, the one mind is also infinitely conscious of conditioned existence.

(a) Each individual consciousness is a unique and equally valuable frame of reference through which that experiences and lives this. There are an infinite number of ways for mind in its unconditioned, non-existent state to experience conditioned existence, across an infinite duration of time. All of conditioned existence is the living expression of that.

(b) Matter is an aspect of the universal mind which forms the background against which the individual consciousness experiences conditioned existence. The world of nature functions as the merely objective framework within which 'I' live 'my' life. Illusorily perceived, understood and experienced as objective reality, the natural world provides an external frame of reference to the relative individual consciousness.

In the transcendental state necessary for this second formless absorption, matter is known as the direct manifestation of mind in its first conditioned reflex of clarity, wisdom and delight in what is. Although everywhere suffused with potential for consciousness, matter is the primal and inherently unconscious expression of <u>that</u> in <u>this</u>. <u>This</u> arises as matter, which unfolds and develops according to the inherent explicate and implicate laws, as the thought process of <u>that</u> unfolds and develops.

(c) Arising from matter, sentient life came into being as the condition of time unfolded its power. Sentient life and inanimate matter have a common source in mind in its formless and unconditioned state. Originally, sentient life was one with matter, experiencing intuitive understanding of the inherent unity of all of conditioned existence.

With the passage of ages, sentient life lost its harmonious realisation of the inherent unity of <u>this</u> and <u>that</u>. As sentient life became absorbed in conditioned existence, rather than in the awareness of <u>this</u> and <u>that</u> as being eternally and indissolubly intertwined, ignorance of <u>that</u> and desire for <u>this</u> grew hand-in-hand. The frame of reference for consciousness shifted gradually and imperceptibly from <u>that</u> to <u>this</u>, and the illusion of the separateness of people and things became dominant.

As ignorance of the nature of reality grows, the law of karma comes into effect. <u>This</u> is in the process of evolving spontaneously, across the ages, towards conscious re-unification with <u>that</u>. The cycle of individual birth, ageing, suffering, death and rebirth unfolds endlessly, until ignorance is overcome and reality is known in its true, final and absolute nature.

Become absorbed in the base consisting of nothingness.

Leaving behind perceptions of infinite consciousness, become aware of nothingness. Experienced and known with the fully enlightened mind, this is known in its true nature as relative and so lacking in absolute reality. Nothing which exists, nothing in conditioned existence, has any absolute reality.

That is pure 'I-am'-ness; mind in its absolute state is expressed in religious terms as the being of God – I am that I am. That is devoid of conditioned quality or activity, being pure, clear, serene, unconditioned, free and blissfully self-aware. In our true nature, each one of us is that and that alone.

Any aspect of life which is not experienced as that is relative, and so unreal and illusory; God alone is, and everything which occurs is God. Underlying all of life is its inherent emptiness or nothingness; God alone is the doer of activity – our minds and bodies are but vehicles for the divine will. The suffering in one's life seems real when experienced from the relative, individual and separate viewpoint. The unreality of life's terrible suffering is only understood once it has been witnessed from the absolute viewpoint.

In the same way, the nothingness or void underlying life can only be experienced and understood from the absolute viewpoint. The transcendent and divine nature of life's ultimate emptiness is found in the enlightened experience of everyday life, knowing that the individual focus of experience is ultimately non-existent. From the absolute point of view of the transcendentally realised mind, conditioned existence is known in its true nature as mere appearance, given the illusion of substance and reality by unenlightened ignorance of its dream-like nature.

Despite the unreality of the world when experienced from the absolute point of view, the undeniable suffering of countless individuals continues as long as they remain locked in relative and unenlightened perspectives. Unreal as this suffering is, enlightenment is the only refuge from the endless cycle of birth, ageing, suffering and death. Implicate Technology is only one of many, many valid paths to release from the suffering inherent in conditioned existence.

When in the highest states of yogic awareness of the nature of reality, the enlightened mind is untainted and undisturbed by its own or another's suffering. Perceiving the universal and all-embracing compassion suffusing the world, Act so as to ease the world's pain. Teach the world to know the true nature of reality, with respect and tolerance for the relative validity of each model of reality.

Become absorbed in the base consisting of neither perception nor non-perception.

Leaving behind perceptions of nothingness, become aware of neither perception nor non-perception. Reality known through the senses is not different from transcendental, trans-sensual being. This and that are ever one and indistinguishable; God is the world.

From the relative point of view, this is undoubtedly tangible and real. From the absolute point of view, conditioned existence has only relative and illusory reality. From the perspective of the fully enlightened person, either or both of these points of view can be experienced as true.

This understood and experienced as that is absolutely real. The world understood and experienced as the will of God is absolutely real. The universe is real if perceived as Brahman. The *Samsara* is real if experienced as *Nirvana*.

The illusory temporal, conditioned reality is real if understood and directly experienced as the manifest form of absolute, unconditioned reality. Fully enlightened, serene and clear, this is known to you in its true nature as the moment-by-moment expression of the infinite harmony of that. There is no distinction possible between God and the world – they are one and the same.

Fully enlightened, knowing through experience both the relative and absolute nature of conditioned existence, understanding the unity of the relative and the absolute, you live now as a conscious part of the universal purpose. Great in yourself, one with that and one with this, live your life without individual and self-willed purpose, fulfilling the karma of your body with humble acceptance. Knowing the divine nature of ordinary everyday life, go as karma bids you to teach the suffering and unenlightened the nature of reality, according to your gifts.

Appendix 1: How to recognise a fully developed model of reality

When a new model of reality with the inherent potential to be widely accepted evolves in any culture, it is the result of preparatory activities of karma across many generations of incarnations. To those who are most prepared, neither the coming of the model nor its content is unexpected, only its form of expression is unanticipated; to those who are ill-prepared, to those whose who are immersed in attachment to conditioned existence, the appearance of a new model of reality is as if from nowhere. As the adherents of a new model of reality grow in number, and so in influence, there is a tendency for them to conflict with the adherents of the prevailing model of reality.

What are the roots of Implicate Technology?

The unified, coherent and structured system of meditation which forms the body of Implicate Technology meditative practice had its origin long before our earliest recorded history. In the West, a generally accessible description of these intuitively-based meditative disciplines has not been available. Conversely, in the East, the history of yoga has been traced back much farther than is possible when using the tools and methodologies of explicate, intellectually-based disciplines.

Up to the attainment of the first stage of enlightenment, the Implicate Technology meditative system is based on Chinese Taoist teachings[1]. The teaching on the second to the fourth stages of enlightenment is based on Tibetan Buddhist yoga[2]. The modes of expression used in

---

[1] See chapter 1, *Beyond the personality: the beginner's guide to enlightenment.*

[2] Evans-Wentz W. Y.; *Tibetan Yoga and Secret Doctrines*; Oxford, Oxford University Press, 1967, pages 101–153.

Implicate Technology to describe the experience of enlightenment owe a strong debt to Indian Hinduism[1].

Implicate Technology clearly acknowledges its debt to the practices and experience of these earlier models of reality. Equally, it should be clearly understood that Implicate Technology is not simply an amalgam of pre-existing Eastern meditative techniques. Yoga transcends all cultural barriers and histories, being the exclusive preserve of none.

The experience and lessons of the highly developed Eastern implicate technology systems are utilised and expressed by Implicate Technology in a context adapted to the demands of late-twentieth century Western secular culture. These Implicate Technology teachings are the systematic and coherent record of contemporary experience on the path to the final stage of enlightenment. Their purpose is to guide and assist others on the far journey along the path to enlightenment.

The Eastern models of reality reflect an awareness that the journey to enlightenment can take many, many lifetimes. Implicate Technology acknowledges the truth of this, and recognises the novelty of such a perspective in our materialistic Western culture. Up to the late-twentieth century, we in the West have lacked the generally accessible cultural perspective necessary to be at ease with the idea of an evolutionary journey across many lifetimes. However, we have been prepared by the evolutionary pattern of karma for a sudden, widespread quantum leap in spiritual development in this generation of incarnations.

Be assured: from the day you start meditating until the day you realise the final stage of enlightenment, the total time elapsed can be as little as eighteen months. To travel this path, from ordinary consciousness to realisation of the unity of reality, in such a short time requires wholehearted dedication and commitment to the practice of these teachings. By meditating as instructed, and so releasing the experience of previous incarnations, you will spontaneously find out how far along the path you have already travelled in previous incarnations.

As well as having roots in Eastern meditative systems, this Western model of reality is also rooted in the Jewish mystical tradition. Developing separately from the mainstream of Jewish culture, the Kabbalah has flowered over the centuries. Splendid in its vision, the Kabbalah has evolved into a fully developed model of reality.

---

[1] Godman, David; *Be As You Are: the Teachings of Sri Ramana Maharshi*; London, Arkana, 1985.

The Kabbalah's greatest achievement has been to identify, in Jewish mystical terminology, "the ten energy-essences that are ..... in constant interplay and underlie all of the universe"[1]. These energy essences, known as the ten *sefirot*, can be diagrammatically represented in the Kabbalistic Tree of Life. By means of this diagrammatic technique, the Kabbalah is able to model, analyse and understand any situation in terms of the interactions of the ten *sefirot*.

The ten conditions of Implicate Technology, which are in constant interplay and underlie all of everyday experience, are, simply, the ten *sefirot* writ large. The ten conditions are an articulation of the same vision which developed the ten *sefirot*, expressed in terms more generally accessible. The ten conditions are the ten *sefirot* translated from the framework and language of Jewish mysticism into the language used by ordinary, intelligent people in the context of their everyday lives.

Rooted in direct experience of the true, final and absolute nature of reality, Implicate Technology clearly acknowledges the similarity of its structure to other models of reality. Apart from personal preference and cultural relevance, there is no inherent advantage of any one fully developed model of reality over another. The ultimate truth is inexpressible, and any model of its nature must necessarily be conditioned and relative.

☆ ☆ ☆ ☆

What are the basic structures to which all fully developed models of reality conform, to a greater or lesser degree?

There are an enormous number of models of reality available to us, ranging from primitive belief systems, through the whole range of contemporary religious systems and cults, to the sophisticated, meditation-based systems of the East. The apparent diversity of forms, terms used and practices is overwhelming. As a result of this complexity and confusion, there is very little communication and understanding evident between the practitioners and believers of the various models of reality.

Faced with this diversity and seeming chaos, the average Westerner seeking to understand the nature and meaning of life is unable to derive

---

[1] Hoffman, Edward; *The Way of Splendour: Jewish Mysticism and Modern Psychology*; Boulder, Shambhala,1981; page 234.

much value from such choice. Believers in every model of reality claim to have the truth; some even claim to possess sole access to the truth. How is one to discern between ignorance, perhaps disguised as an influential and powerful religion, and a fully developed model of reality?

In fact, the apparent diversity of spiritual and religious expression can be reduced to a limited number of forms. Actually, there are four generic paths to enlightenment. All models of reality shape themselves naturally round one or more of these four fundamental ways of understanding the nature of reality.

A fully developed model of reality will both describe the true nature of reality and provide devotional or meditative practices to assist the individual to realise the inexpressible truth of reality. Although the language and the practices used will vary according to time and place, every fully realised spiritual system maps a path to enlightenment. When the seeker possesses a knowledge of the structure common to all models of reality sufficient to be able to identify a model most suitable to that individual's particular needs, then there can be true choice.

A widely accessible exposition of the common patterns underlying the superficial diversity of the many models of reality currently available will open up the possibility for those who utilise the different religious and spiritual models to communicate on a clear and equal basis. Clear in the knowledge of what leads to understanding of the absolute and what merely perpetuates ignorance of the true nature of reality, it becomes possible to distinguish between partially developed and fully developed models of reality. With a clear and shared understanding of both the superficial differences and the common elements of each model, users of fully developed models of reality need no longer vie with each other for spiritual, or even temporal, authority.

Authority in spiritual matters need not necessarily come from a recognised figurehead, though such a person may indeed have author-ity. True authority in spiritual matters results from direct intuitive experience of the absolute. With a clear understanding of the absolute nature of reality, it becomes possible to tell the difference between dogma and knowledge based on experience.

The four paths to enlightenment are the four fundamental forms of yoga – devotion to God, knowledge of reality, the way of action, and spiritual disciplining of the body and its energy systems. Through meditating on the discussion of these paths which follows, you should be able to discern the underlying form of any religious or spiritual system. Those elements of a model of reality which reflect one or more of these paths lead to enlightenment. Those which do not are products of ignorance and perpetuate bondage to birth, ageing, suffering and death.

☆   ☆   ☆   ☆

What are the primary points of similarity between Implicate Technology and the existing Eastern models of reality?

Implicate Technology is a Western-originated model of reality, reflecting the experiences, and adapted to the needs, of everyday Western life. The language of Implicate Technology largely comprises words used in ordinary life. There are, however, three exceptions – three Sanskrit terms imported from Eastern implicate technology systems and used freely in Implicate Technology.

This sparse use of the rich and fruitful language of the Eastern implicate technologies is deliberate. Implicate Technology is not a hybrid of various Eastern systems, relying for its authority on the ancient authority of the venerable Eastern technologies. Rather, Implicate Technology is a spontaneous evolution of Western spiritual understanding, relying for its authority on the depth of spiritual experience it provides for those who practise its meditative techniques.

We in the West are subject to a form of spiritual imperialism, which is the analogue of the commercial imperialism through which the West still exploits and ransacks the East. Sensing the failure of the currently available Western religious and spiritual systems, many in the West have adopted wholeheartedly the methods and beliefs of Eastern systems. This transportation of the spiritual products of one culture to another is rarely harmonious or successful.

The East has sensed this deep need in the West, and we have seen an influx of representatives of Eastern models of reality seeking to persuade us of the value of their systems. Aware of the authority and accuracy of the various systems they represent, they come to the West in genuine humility to try to bring us the benefits of spiritual civilisation. Quite unconsciously, they also condescend to us, as they treat us like the spiritually backward peoples we actually are.

Much thoughtfulness, consideration and caution is necessary when attempts are made to introduce products of implicate or explicate technologies from a culture developed in the use of these products into a culture unused to and unprepared for them. Just as the villager in a less developed part of India has no application for cheap mass-produced personal computers, so, too, the average spiritually impoverished Western city-dweller has no appetite for highly sophisticated meditative systems. Economically impoverished and subject to disease from unsanitary conditions, the Indian villager needs a clean fresh supply of water, a simple reliable means of producing cheap electricity and an understanding of basic health care and nutrition. Spiritually impoverished and subject to disease from an environment polluted by ignorance of the organic unity of reality, the Western city-dweller needs pure and simple meditative exercises to deal with Western experiences and perceptions of reality.

Without a sense of equality and shared responsibility, cultures simply exploit and damage each other as they barter the products of implicate and explicate technologies. The poorly paid worker in the East spends relatively large amounts of money on useless products of Western explicate technology such as heavily advertised, manufactured, soft drinks, instead of consuming the traditional, cheaper and more nutritious local alternatives. The spiritually ignorant Westerner, desperate for fulfilment and meaning in life, has a tendency to become absorbed into wholly inappropriate Eastern-based spiritual systems, resulting in much unhappiness both to the seeker and to his or her family and friends, from whom there can soon be estrangement.

If such destructive imbalances in cultural trading patterns are to be effectively dealt with, we need to develop ways to discuss, analyse and understand the interactions between the various dominant models of reality. Such a politics of transcendence requires a basic understanding of the elements and practices common to all fully developed models of reality. With a knowledge and understanding of the roots common to all implicate technologies, it becomes possible to recognise and respect cultural differences on the basis of a shared sense of fundamental equality.

Implicate Technology imports only three fundamental Sanskrit terms from Eastern models of reality – karma, yoga and samadhi. A term for the fundamental implicate law known as karma, for the practical implicate disciplines known collectively as yoga, and for the state of undistracted alertness known as samadhi, in which the implicate nature of reality is consciously and continuously experienced, must exist in any fully developed model of reality. Implicate Technology uses the ancient and well suited language of Sanskrit for these terms in order to emphasise the common ground between this Western model of reality and the older Eastern paths to understanding the spiritual truths underlying material reality.

What are the primary characteristics of the four generic paths to enlightenment?

The path of devotion, known in the East as bhakti yoga, is the most common, and for many the least difficult, way to enlightenment. Calling on humanity's innate capacity to act out of love of an ideal, the way of devotion leads to enlightenment through the unremitting dedication of every aspect of one's life to the chosen ideal. This ideal is usually, but not necessarily, God.

Possessed by devotion to the ideal, the individual mind gradually loses its attachment to the external and internal stimuli which normally preoccupy consciousness. Simultaneously, attachment to the ideal grows until it becomes the one-pointed focus of the aspirant's consciousness. With the arising of the capacity for one-pointed concentration, the individual dwells on the ideal with undistracted alertness.

The sustained experience of undistracted alertness, or samadhi, leads to dissolution of the illusion of individuality and separation. Attraction to and desire for the fruits of material existence fall away, and the mind re-unites with its ideal. Aware of the divine unity of all that exists, the fully realised follower of the path of devotion exists only to dedicate every thought and act, with unremitting perseverance, to the service of the ideal. This ideal is usually God, but it can also be devotion to humanity in general, devotion to a person who embodies realisation of the final stage of enlightenment, or even devotion to an ideal of ethics or beauty.

The path of knowledge of the nature of reality, known in the East as jnana yoga, is the foundation of this Implicate Technology meditative system. Calling on the inherent desire to understand the nature of reality and the true nature of one's experience of life, the way of knowledge leads to enlightenment through unremitting dedication to understanding every aspect of one's life as a meaningful part of a unified whole. The unified whole which is reality can be understood from one viewpoint as a process apparent only to the transcendentally realised mind, and from another viewpoint as the manifest form of God.

Possessed by the desire to understand and integrate into reality, the individual mind first analyses itself and then analyses the nature of the external world. As the mind's capacity to function at transcendental levels of consciousness awakens, the underlying nature of mind and matter becomes apparent. Both the individual mind which experiences and the apparently objective world which is experienced are understood in their true nature as relative manifestations of the one absolute mind which alone is.

The way of devotion and the way of knowledge are two different approaches to the same goal: both paths lead to transcendental realisation of the unified and integrated nature of perceptible reality. Once the illusury sense of specific individuality has been transcended, it a only a matter of personal taste whether reality is experienced as unity with God or as an inherently unified process. To the transcendentally realised mind, capable of experiencing reality simultaneously from relative and absolute viewpoints, the difference between the way of knowledge and the way of devotion is simply one of individual temperament and perspective.

The way of knowledge of reality and the way of devotion to an ideal intertwine, according to one's individuality and circumstances, and both paths find common ground in **the way of action**, known as karma yoga in the East. We live in the world and must necessarily act in it—karma yoga is the path of acting as an expression of divine or transcendent will, rather than acting as an expression of individual will. Implicate Technology teaches that the way of knowledge and the way of action are intertwined at every step along the path.

The culmination of karma yoga is effortless action. To the transcendentally realised mind, every action is understood and experienced as being a product of the spontaneous flow of reality, or God's will, and not as an act of individual choice. One who has experienced the absolute nature of reality is capable of acting without the mind triggering the karmically reactive system which dominates unenlightened consciousnesses.

The fourth path to enlightenment is **the way of the body**, known in the East as hatha yoga. This way utilises a profound understanding of the body's inherent implicate energy systems to bring about progress towards the final stage of enlightenment. By combining physical postures and exercises with an understanding of the relationship between breathing and states of consciousness, progress can be made along the path to realising the absolute nature of reality.

104

We in the West have not yet developed a sufficient understanding of the implicate nature of reality to be capable of producing a fully realised form of hatha yoga. The yoga of sexual energy taught in chapter 5 of *The beginner's guide to enlightenment* bears the same relationship to a fully developed hatha yoga as gunpowder does to a nuclear warhead. The yoga of sexual energy taught in Implicate Technology is only a starting point for the understanding of the body's inherent implicate energy systems.

☆   ☆   ☆   ☆

What are the characteristics of a fully developed model of reality?

If you are motivated to overcome your inherent ignorance of the nature of reality, it is very important to understand the characteristics of a fully developed model of reality. The model you choose to work with to overcome your ignorance and its attendant endless re-iteration of the process of birth, ageing, sorrow and death is a matter of circumstances and personal inclination. If the model does not reflect the true nature of reality, you will not become enlightened and you will remain eternally locked into the karmically active system of learning through suffering.

A fully developed model of reality provides the user with a path which leads from the initial state of ignorance of the true nature of all that is experienced to enlightened understanding through experience of the final and absolute nature of reality. Such a spiritual system will provide practical meditational or devotional techniques to effect the necessary transformations in consciousness. It will provide a framework, in a series of graded practical techniques and exercises, to enable the user accurately to determine both the current level of consciousness and the next step along the path.

When you work within the guiding structure of a fully developed model of reality which is appropriate to your individual and cultural requirements, then you can be confident that your use of the model will lead you to enlightenment. All that is required is that you diligently practise the appropriate meditative or devotional techniques, while understanding your life in the context of the teachings. A life lived in harmony with the moral structure inherent in conditioned existence *and* a mind working under appropriate guidance to divest itself of ignorance of the nature of reality lead inevitably to enlightenment.

All fully developed models of reality reflect the underlying structure of conditioned existence, each using language and imagery appropriate to its particular cultural environment. The method of approach and point of view vary from model to model. Only the following elements, which combine with different emphasis according to the evolutionary requirements of karma, remain constant in the process of becoming enlightened.

<u>That</u>/ God/ Brahman/ The Void/ Tao/ etc.

Every fully developed model of reality talks of material reality, discernible by the five senses, and of the non-material source of that reality. When the model has been fully understood through experience by the user, the apparent separation and duality between tangible reality and its simultaneously immanent and transcendent source is experienced as a unity. The primary purpose of the model is to effect that unity, through the evolutionary development of individual and collective consciousness.

Karma/ Destiny/ God's Will/ Tao/ etc.

All fully articulated spiritual systems describe a natural force which brings about consequences appropriate to each individual's thoughts and actions. This irresistible force is frequently described in the form of an implacable judge who dispenses appropriate rewards and punishments, often after death. This force cannot be defied: the individual must experience the consequences of unenlightened behaviour in this life, in the after-death state or in the lives to come.

Morality

Humanity's need for moral systems to provide guidance in daily living is due to an unconscious awareness of the karmically reactive nature of reality. All visions of reality stemming from the experience of enlightened minds describe a way of behaving which minimises the incurring of negative compensating reactions from reality. Each moral system originated by an enlightened person is an attempt to guide others safely to realisation of the true, final and absolute nature of reality.

Suffering

Suffering is an inescapable part of incarnate experience. All fully unfolded descriptions of reality point out the educational nature of suffering. Properly understood within the context of a realised model of reality, suffering directs you to understand both your own nature and the nature of reality. Unenlightened ignorance of the true nature of ordinary experience only compounds and extends your suffering. The only sure escape from this inevitable suffering is through enlightenment.

Ignorance/maya/enlightenment

Fully realised models of reality exist to lead us from ignorance of the nature of reality to enlightenment about our own nature. Living in the ignorance of unenlightenment means living a life enmeshed in a web of illusion. Only enlightenment can dispel that illusion, as awakening from a dream brings knowledge that all that was experienced was the product of the dreaming mind, and only enlightenment can reveal the true, final and absolute nature of reality.

Reincarnation

Any fully developed model of reality, in teaching awareness of the true nature and purpose of life, must necessarily provide guidance on reincarnation. Repeated rebirth is a function of ignorance of the nature of reality. Reincarnation necessarily occurs endlessly until enlightenment provides release from the repetitive cycle of birth, ageing, suffering and death.

Yoga

Yoga is the generic name for the practical techniques which lead from ignorance to enlightenment. A fully developed model of reality will supply at least one coherent, structured system of yoga which can lead the practitioner to enlightenment. Such a yoga will always teach a practical path to the reunion of the individual mind with the immanent and transcendent source of material reality.

Samadhi/undistracted alertness/altered states of mind

All fully developed models of reality provide guidance on how to achieve the transformations of consciousness necessary to move from ordinary awareness to enlightenment. The experience of deepest samadhi, or undistracted alertness in focusing consciousness on the absolute source of perceptible reality, is necessary before enlightenment can be attained. With the sustained and effortless experience of undistracted alertness, ignorance is washed away and truth alone is understood through direct intuitive experience.

What are the limitations of contemporary Christianity as a fully developed model of reality?

Over millennia, the East has had a proliferation of models of reality – that is to say, there exist in the East extensive oral and written records of the systemised experiences of individuals on the path to enlightenment. When a fresh experience of the absolute nature of reality arises in the East, as a result of the evolutionary activity of karma, the newly enlightened person, if empowered and made articulate by karma to speak directly and clearly to the surrounding culture, can relate the new teaching to the existing spiritual systems. For much of the East, the ancient Sanskrit language forms the basis of the culturally accepted models of the implicate structure of reality, against which any new experience and articulation of the absolute will be measured and tested.

From the point of view of the aspirant struggling against the mind's accumulated ignorance to attain enlightenment, the pre-existing models of reality serve as a map. These systematic and structured records of previous spiritual journeys help the traveller in consciousness to identify the major experiences, and provide sound advice on how to understand and transcend each stage until the final goal is reached and the journey ceases. Properly and wisely used, such guidance enables the traveller to journey with greater safety and speed towards realisation of the absolute through direct experience.

From the point of view of the newly enlightened person struggling to articulate experiences which can only crudely be put into words, the existing models of reality enable the realised mind to compare and contrast contemporarily relevant ways of expressing the experiences encountered along the path. The availability of comparable models of reality is of great importance in providing a stabilising perspective on a newly emerging spiritual system. Fresh and culturally stimulating visions of reality only arise occasionally in history, as part of the fall and rise in a culture's spiritual development.

Consider carefully the origins of Christianity, in terms of the availability of comparable spiritual systems. Jesus had only the study of Jewish scriptures, for a comparative experiential map, to guide him and assist him in articulating his inner experience of the absolute in terms accessible to his contemporaries. The scriptures indicated clearly and unequivocally the terrible role which the awaited Messiah would have to fulfil.

The gospels abound with examples of Jesus's concern to comply with the authority of the Jewish scriptures, so that the ancient prophecies might be fulfilled. The events of his ministry had been foretold in detail, that is to say, his actions were culturally expected and predetermined. Jesus carefully and deliberately set out on the path to crucifixion, so that the words of the prophets would come true.

The Jewish spiritual system, as discussed in chapter 2 of this book, marked the first culture-wide attempt in Western consciousness to express the experience of reality as a unified whole. From the vantage point of later millennia, the Jewish model can be seen as a first attempt by Western consciousness to produce a fully developed model of reality. Jesus's task was to refine and develop that map. His task was to show in greater detail the path to the goal and the nature of the goal itself.

Lacking the extensive range of comparative teachings which we in the West have had available to us in the twentieth century, Jesus had to rely for guidance on the available teachings based on the Jewish scriptures, and on his own experiences on the path to enlightenment. As a result of this, key aspects of his teaching were formulated in the limited terms of Jewish Palestinian culture of two thousand years ago. Jesus taught that the kingdom of heaven was to be gained solely through belief in him and his teaching. Central to the difficulties facing contemporary Christianity is the unwillingness of many ordinary people to accept Jesus as the sole authority and means of access to God.

The situation of profound and widespread ignorance of comparative spiritual systems which existed at the time of the origins of Christianity is at the root of the misconception distorting Jesus's original teaching. Jesus taught that he was the sole source of access to God because, quite simply, in the limited context of his time and place, he really was the sole point of access. In the overall context of humanity's progressive development of models of reality, Jesus can clearly be seen as one enlightened teacher among many.

The next major area of difficulty for contemporary Christianity is its insistence on belief in Jesus as a prerequisite for experience of the kingdom of God. Jesus had undoubtedly travelled along the path to the final stage of enlightenment; but it is clear from the evidence in the gospels that he was unable to teach, except privately to his disciples, the direct experience of the kingdom of heaven[1]. This does not suggest a limitation in Jesus's ability as a teacher; rather, it indicates a limitation

---

[1]   Matthew 13, 10-11; Mark 4, 10-11, 34.

in the culture he was working in at that place and time.

Belief in spiritual matters is only necessary, for an individual or a culture, when direct intuitive experience is not possible. In that culture of two thousand years ago, which was taking the first steps in the lengthy transition of Western civilisation into an ethically-based civilisation, widespread direct experience of the absolute nature of reality was not possible. Where a society has not yet evolved sufficiently to have produced a fully developed model of reality, the only way for most individuals to access spiritual truths is through belief in another person's direct intuitive experience.

Jesus taught that he was the sole source of access to God and that salvation lay in belief in him, because in the limited terms of his relatively unevolved culture that was the literal truth. The need for belief in Jesus remained strong for as long as Christianity fulfilled its karmic function of evolving Western civilisation into an ethically-based culture. The capacity of individuals to be satisfied, through belief, about the truth behind Jesus's teachings, waned correspondingly as the civilising effect of his message achieved the necessary moral evolution in Western consciousness.

This process of Western culture evolving spontaneously towards a spiritually-based civilisation has as its inevitable consequence the growing realisation that, for increasing numbers of individuals, belief of itself is no longer sufficient to satisfy their spiritual aspirations. Fully developed spiritual understanding is not possible if it is based merely on belief. Direct intuitive experience of the nature of reality is the key to a mature spiritual understanding.

As all who have such intuitive knowledge agree, the direct experience of the absolute nature of reality is inexpressible. The absolute is pure experience of being, transcending any conditioned modes of expression. Any teacher must articulate the inexpressible in fresh, contemporary terms, in order to help others along the path.

It is impossible for any teacher to describe a detailed and systematic path leading to direct experience of the absolute without incorporating both an individual and a cultural bias into the descriptive system. That bias may not be apparent to the teacher's contemporaries, since they share the cultural bias, and the teaching will seem new and revelatory to them. As the relevance of a teaching fades with the passage of time, its limitations become apparent. As a spiritual system becomes less relevant to the way people live their lives, and less able to address and satisfy their need for inner growth, so do its limitations become clear.

110

The individual bias shows in the choice of theistic or purely transcendental modes of description of the absolute. The true, final and absolute nature of reality can be accurately described both as God, and as mind in its unconditioned state, devoid of qualities. God is the first reflex in conditioned existence of mind in its unconditioned form – God and mind in its unconditioned state are one and inseparable.

The cultural bias shows in the structural detail of the system of expression. The language and concepts used, and the experiences discussed, all reflect the need for development in consciousness of a particular culture over a particular time. The only unshakeable absolute in any spiritual system is the inexpressible, pure and all-embracing goal, knowable only by direct intuitive experience; all else in any model of reality is only relative in nature and has only temporary cultural validity.

Jesus taught his understanding of the absolute nature of reality in theistic terms, because it suited both his nature and the needs of his contemporaries. Why did Jesus choose to represent his experience of the absolute in the male imagery of God the Father? The answer is certainly not because God, the first reflex of the one mind in its unconditioned state, is male.

It makes as much sense to talk of God the Mother as it does to talk of God the Father. Neither view is more true than the other, although one view may be more relevant in particular circumstances to particular people.

Teaching in terms of God the Father was the natural extension of the traditional Jewish patriarchal symbolism which existed in the male-dominated culture of Palestine two thousand years ago. By adopting and expressing anew the existing cultural points of reference, Jesus was able to reach the greatest number of people with his teaching. To teach of God the Mother would have been meaningless in that particular historical context.

The male-orientated, early Christian model of reality was also characterised by an aversion to woman's sexuality, which was to be contained and controlled inside an allegedly God-ordained marriage (children, for the procreation of). The Christian notions of God as male and of marriage sanctified by religion as the sole legitimate arena for sexual experience, have been treated as absolute products of divine wisdom, although only based on the relative authority of Jesus and the disciples. In this way views relevant to and originated in a particular culture two thousand years ago, have been passed down to our profoundly different culture as unshakeable holy writ.

111

As such rigid religious attitudes become increasingly irrelevant to the way the majority of people live their lives, the inevitable reaction sets in. The power and influence of the Christian Church is waning where it fails to adapt to the rapid changes in people's thinking. Generally speaking, Christian Churches have lost sight of the freshness and vitality of Jesus's original teaching.

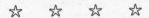

How can the committed and dedicated Christian attain enlightenment using this secular Implicate Technology meditative system?

God's love permeates and sustains this world. This experience of infinite and all-embracing love is characteristic of the fully enlightened mind, when inclined towards a devotional path. Temperamentally inclined to worship the divine which is inherent in perceptible reality, the aspirant works towards the goal of realising the transcendent re-unification with God, whose nature is love.

The practical path by which the committed Christian can attain the transcendent re-unification with God is the same as for anyone else. The simple meditation on breathing taught in *The beginner's guide to enlightenment* forms the basis for the first transformation of consciousness. All that is required, in addition to committed daily practice, is an understanding of the process in terms of Christian concepts.

From the Christian perspective, the many trials experienced during the period of karmic testing preceding the attainment of the first stage of enlightenment can be understood as tests to establish whether you are pure enough to be worthy of God's love. God will test your capacity to rise above, and become detached from, your own desires. The Implicate Technology teaching of karma as the purposeful influence in a meaningful and integrated process simply provides a detailed way to discuss the technical mechanism whereby God tests the aspirant for inner purity.

As taught in chapter 2 of this book, before you can attain the experience of samadhi, you must set your life in harmony with the moral pattern inherent in the structure of reality. Samadhi, or the peace that passes all understanding as it is referred to in the Bible, is the result of a life lived in harmony with, and acceptance of, God's loving will. The committed Christian can rely, with confidence, on Jesus's original moral teachings as a guide to morally harmonious living in accordance with the divine will.

Once God's grace has been received through the gift of samadhi, you will be preoccupied with dwelling on the nature of God. Through concentrating, with unwavering determination, on your love of God, you will gain the capacity for one-pointed meditation on God's nature. Sustained experience of undistractedly concentrating on God's nature will reveal the illusory distinction between the lover and the beloved – in truth, you and God have always and only been one.

Once the illusion of individuality and separateness has been dissolved, it will only require sustained one-pointed meditation on the nature of God for the equally illusory barriers of birth and ageing, suffering and death to fall away. Alternatively, you may choose to follow the detailed Implicate Technology meditations in chapters 4 and 5, substituting 'Godhead' for '<u>that</u>' and substituting 'God' for 'wisdom, clarity and delight'. Once you have realised the divine unity of all that exists, you will be as a driverless vehicle dedicated to the service of God's infinite love.

☆   ☆   ☆   ☆

How can committed Christians re-establish the freshness and vitality of Jesus's original teachings?

Seeking God's grace and love, the committed Christian can find direct experience of God through practice of these Implicate Technology meditations from a religious perspective. In due course, God willing, practice of meditation will bring direct, intuitive experience of the divine nature underlying the world of everyday experience. The committed Christian will naturally seek to interpret and understand such experience in terms of Christ's teachings.

The way for the committed Christian to understand the experiences encountered along the path to unity with God is to go back to Jesus's original teachings in the gospels. First, pare away all accretions on Jesus's original teaching, leaving only the record of his sayings. Then, re-interpret the original sayings in the light of what you have learned, through your own experience of meditation within the fully developed framework of Implicate Technology, of the nature and structure of perceptible reality.

The primary purpose of the Implicate Technology meditative system is to teach direct intuitive realisation of the absolute subjectivity of the Godhead. The committed Christian who has attained unity with God through practice of these meditations is capable of producing specifically Christian devotional meditations to help and guide other Christians along the path to God. Implicate Technology is only one of many paths to enlightenment – Christianity will be able to reach out to, and help, far greater numbers of seekers of God's love when its advocates recognise that, like every other model of reality, Christianity is only one of many paths to the eternal truth.

The committed and dedicated Christian, who has experienced the reality of God's all-pervading love and who wishes to express that understanding within the officially approved structures of the Christian hierarchy, can expect severe opposition and obstruction from those in power. As with all bureaucracies which institutionalise an original and great idea, the maintaining of the current power balance within the institution becomes more important than the founding vision. The Christian Church is much more interested in maintaining its social, moral, political and economic influence than it is concerned to spread Jesus's message of universal love.

As well as being preoccupied with maintaining its temporal power base, the Christian Church has a long history of alienating itself from elements essential to any fully developed model of reality. The Second Council of Constantinople, meeting in A. D. 553, anathematised the supporters of reincarnation and karma[1]. The Christian Church officially upholds an incomplete model of reality which cannot, of itself, lead the committed Christian to direct intuitive experience of the unity of humanity and God.

It follows that the committed and dedicated Christian who has direct transcendental experience of the love of God faces an uphill and difficult struggle in attemting to re-introduce the full breadth of Jesus's original vision into the contemporary Church. The Catholic Church has a long history of isolating and excommunicating Christians whose views fall outside of acceptable official norms. The Christian who attempts to breathe relevance and vitality into the temporal power base of Christianity, perhaps by working for the ordination of women in a male-dominated system, will need to move slowly, carefully and cautiously.

Careful study and practice of the power discipline, as taught in chapter 3 of *The beginner's guide to enlightenment*, will enable the Christian seeking to transform the Church from within to deal with obstruction

---

[1] Evans-Wentz, W. Y.; *The Tibetan Book of the Dead*; Oxford, Oxford University Press, 1960; pp 4, 185n, 234-5, 239.

from those in authority. Reality will inevitably unfold in its own way; your task is always to <u>Act</u> in harmony with the flow of reality. The perfect vehicle for God's love knows that all obstructions to unity with God are the will of God, and it is God alone who will deal with those who obstruct across endless lifetimes.

☆   ☆   ☆   ☆

In everyday practical terms, what is the end result of working within the framework of Implicate Technology?

All fully developed models of reality provide a path for the individual to realise the pure, primal and original state of mind which underlies, forms and manifests itself as the process of conditioned existence. All such models provide practical guidance in recognising the illusory nature of individual existence. All such models re-unite the mind with its source.

The major differences between the various fully developed models are best understood as variations in cultural expression. The ultimate truth, being unconditioned and so beyond any form of expression, can be usefully conveyed from any number of points of view. The differences in perspective supplied by the various models of reality are simply a function of the needs of particular cultures over particular time periods.

This Western secular model of reality is direct and highly functional. To find out if it works, sit down and meditate as instructed. <u>Live</u> and <u>Act</u> throughout your life and you will realise the final stage of enlightenment.

Committed daily practice of these Implicate Technology teachings will act as a catalyst in your life. Your inherent ability to function in a positive and healing way will be enhanced as you advance in your practice of meditation. You will become empowered to contribute to the development of your culture, according to the workings of your karma.

Implicate Technology is based on embracing the events of everyday life, not on renouncing everyday concerns. This teaching produces individuals who are fully integrated into ordinary, everyday life. This secular model of reality produces cultural activists, not religious leaders.

Appendix 2: The world-healing process

Empty and powerful, aware of the illusory and non-existent nature of individual life, the enlightened person knows that reality will unfold regardless of individual volition. Dedicated to helping others find release from the relative illusion that suffering is real, through experiencing the freedom of the absolute and the consequent realisation of the ultimate non-existence of suffering, the enlightened person is endlessly committed to a healing course of action. Faced with the ceaseless uncertainties of relative existence, the enlightened person renounces personal control over events and instead relies on meditation-enhanced healing practices to influence the surrounding environment in an impersonal, disinterested and harmonious way.

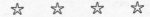

What is the world-healing process?

We live in terrible times.

Our food, air and water are polluted with artificial ingredients. Our natural resources are being abused and squandered on a massive scale. Violence, tension and unrest are increasing everywhere.

There is widespread distrust of leaders in most areas of activity in which our culture engages, particularly distrust of political leaders. Widespread long-term unemployment, and the consequent economic deprivation, threaten to create enormous reservoirs of individual futility and frustration. The gap between the 'haves' and the 'have-nots' grows steadily, both within and between nations.

Our cultural products – written, aural and visual – are increasingly concerned with the superficiality of glamour and outward appearances. New and fresh works of creativity expressing our deepest needs are appearing with increasing rarity. Our values are becoming increasingly shallow and superficial and our art forms in all media reflect this barren and sterile outlook.

On top of all this, we are each subject to the fearful risks of AIDS, terrorism, nuclear war and racial conflict. The world is suffering daily and deeply.

We live in truly terrible times.

The whole of <u>this</u> is formed, structured and shaped by the evolutionary force of karma, so that across unimaginable expanses of time, <u>this</u> develops a fully conscious awareness of its true nature as <u>that</u>.

Know that this desolation and suffering is the result of the cyclic activity of karma, operating on a global basis. Through the decay of our existing social structures and the loss of faith in our existing systems of value, both individually and generally, we are being prepared for the growth of new forms of cultural activity. The old and now sterile ways still hold the power: your task, as a person who has made some progress along the path of understanding the nature of reality through direct experience, is to nurture the growth of new ways of understanding.

Follow the promptings of karma, as you work to introduce changes in your environment according to your individual gifts and abilities. Through your own growth in understanding the nature of reality, help others to revitalise their understanding, whatever their model of reality may be. Give this assistance quietly, modestly, unceremoniously and without desire for personal gain or power.

Be clear: our suffering world will be changed by the steady, unremitting work of people on the path to enlightenment. The contribution of such people to transcending suffering is of prime importance, regardless of whether or not the world recognises or appreciates the effort. Their primary task is to help others to experience for themselves the true and absolute nature of reality.

To introduce others to the standards and values of a way of living based on a deep-seated and genuine experience of the true nature of reality, you must teach through your actions. Convey your understanding of enlightened ways of behaviour by <u>Live</u>-ing and <u>Act</u>ing in your daily life. Teach by example and not just by words.

In addition, you can contribute significantly to easing suffering by practising the world-healing meditation. This practice is unlikely to produce any dramatic short-term benefits. Yet it is a vital component in the process of re-establishing an harmonious balance in our troubled world.

Practicality is the essence of the ordinary Implicate Technology meditative system. At each stage in the meditative process, you can test your progress against given indicators; but such practical tests cannot be applied to the world-healing meditation.

Although possession of faith helps you make progress in the ordinary meditative practices, it is not essential: the key element is to learn from your own experience. This sound principle does not and cannot apply to the world-healing meditation. There is no way for an unenlightened person to make a step-by-step verification of the effectiveness of this meditation.

The proof that the world-healing meditation works is a direct intuitive experience, which is only accessible to a fully enlightened mind. The enlightened mind, contemplating the nature of this meditation, knows that it works. That is the only form of proof available of the validity of this meditation.

A person who has not yet realised the final stage of enlightenment, and who is committed to harmoniously changing the individual and general environment, can only rely on faith as a support in this meditation. From your own experience in the Implicate Technology meditations, you know that they work for you. Accept with unquestioning faith the authority of these teachings on the world-healing meditation, and practise the meditation daily for the benefit of yourself and all others.

If you experience doubt about the practicality and effectiveness of the world-healing meditation, your efforts will prove correspondingly fruitless, according to your degree of doubt. Simply focus your concentration steadily on the meditation and work for the good of yourself and all others. Meditate as directed, with faith, pure and undiluted by doubt.

If emotional or intellectual doubts remain, it is better to have an attitude of indifference rather than to reject outright these teachings on the world-healing meditation. Each one of us can contribute negatively or positively to the process of healing our suffering world. It is better for yourself and for everyone else that you remain indifferent, rather than that you sustain a negative attitude to the process of world-healing.

The world-healing meditation works by progressively neutralising negative karma. Such negative karma has been accumulated both within this lifetime and over many previous lifetimes. This meditation neutralises the negative karma, both of the individual who meditates and of the surrounding environment.

The effects of this meditation depend on the power and purity of the meditator. The cleansing and purifying process first affects the meditator and then the surrounding environment. The more people who practise the world-healing meditation daily, the greater the daily cleansing and purifying effect on our suffering world.

We will yet live in good times. Through daily practice of the world-healing meditation for a minimum of fifteen minutes, both you and your environment will be cleansed, purified and healed of the suffering caused by the accumulation of negative karma. Practise and teach the world-healing meditation with unquestioning faith, and we will yet live in happier times.

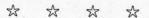

What can you do to assist in the struggle against AIDS?

The rise and spread of AIDS is a function of the sickness and aridity of our time. We have, collectively, lost contact with the healing powers inherent in fully realised models of reality. In the widest sense, we have lost sight of our roots in <u>that</u> – as a result, we are sick and the sickness manifests as AIDS, as well as other horrors.

The morally crippled, who in our society include many religious extremists and sexual bigots, have a tendency to put the blame for causing AIDS on those who suffer AIDS. Those who seize on the rise of AIDS to enforce their prejudices against the sexual activities of others will, inevitably, incur negative karmic consequences in this life or one of the lives to come. What is required to deal with AIDS is not divisive moral bigotry and complacency, but compassionate activity directed at individual and cultural healing.

AIDS is a moral issue in the widest sense of enforcing our cultural awakening to the unified nature of reality. One way or another, AIDS will touch everybody's life in the late-twentieth century. Quite simply, AIDS hammers home the point that, underlying our apparent separation and isolation from each other, our lives are all connected.

The only safe cure for AIDS lies in the development of meditation-enhanced healing techniques. Dedicated meditative practice will bring about the profound changes in attitude necessary to inhibit the progress of the virus, both in individual cases and in general. Mere treatment of the physical symptoms alone, without such a profound change in inner orientation, will inevitably fail to heal the whole person.

The meditative techniques of Implicate Technology, or of any other fully developed model of reality, allied to an understanding of the integrated and unified nature of the human psycho-physiological system, offer the best approach to mitigating or curing AIDS. Research into this area can be undertaken by individuals or small groups, without dependence on the chemicals and equipment produced by our expensive and dangerous Western explicate medicines and their associated industries. Practice of the world-healing meditation, as taught at the end of this chapter, will enable you to contribute positively to the struggle against AIDS.

AIDS is a problem we all face – East and West, black and white, rich and poor, heterosexual and homosexual, male and female. AIDS transcends any of the artificial and divisive boundaries humanity has imposed on itself. When we learn to accept and express our needs through unifying and fully developed models of reality, then the karmic causes of AIDS will gradually cease to be active.

The root cause of AIDS is the widespread cultural and individual disharmony resulting from our fragmented and divisive views of the world. Immersed in a futile quest for individual fulfilment through material prosperity and sensual pleasures alone, our cultural values have led us to widespread conflict and division. This disharmony in our lives has evolved into the matrix of unhealthy lifestyles and barren attitudes which encourage the AIDS virus to flourish. The root cure for AIDS is the individual and cultural harmony which will result from the widespread acceptance of integrated and unifying worldviews.

Follow your intuition, as you engage in the world-healing process to heal yourself and others.

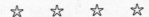

What can the ordinary person do to assist in the struggle against terrorism?

Every event, however terrible or savage it may appear, occurs through the infinite compassion inherent in <u>this</u>. Witness and understand the horror of terrorism, with the clear and certain knowledge that it is not possible for an act of terrorism to remain unpunished. Karma ensures that the perpetrators of terrorism, and those who assist terrorists, incur corrective and balancing experiences in this life, the after-death state or in any of the lives to come.

Terrorism is an act of violence committed for political purposes by lawfully appointed or self-appointed individuals, groups or bodies, and is perpetrated on those deemed by the perpetrators to be legitimate targets. An act of violence committed by one armed force on another is ordinary human stupidity and not an act of terrorism. Severe karmic penalties will be incurred by those who commit the act of terrorist violence, those who assist, and those who create the climate of authorisation for such violence.

The manifest injustice and consequent violence of late-twentieth century life is the product of collective karmic consequences incurred over many, many previous generations of incarnations. The prevalence of violence as an accepted expression of political will is a product of our widespread lack of understanding of fully developed models of reality. Having lost sight of our inherent unity, we rend and tear apart the lives of others in the vain hope of fulfilling our own.

Your problem is this: how can you, as an individual, contribute to the end of terrorism? What can you do to stop the actions of anonymous cells of self-appointed killers, or to stop the vast apparatus of state terrorism which is utilised in oppressive wars and repression? How can you alter the destructive nature of forces over which you have no direct control, but which can arbitrarily seize on you as a 'legitimate' target for violence?

Know as a certainty that all occurrences are subject to karma. Even after you have attained the freedom of the final stage of enlightenment, know that only your mind will be freed from the karmically reactive system and not your body. Your body remains subject to karma.

Within this context, the one power you do possess to pit against harsh external forces is the mind's inherent ability to purify and cleanse itself of accumulated negative karma. If you set about doing this as instructed at the end of this chapter, you will begin to purge your own negative karma. With sufficient effort, the beneficial effects will also spread into your surrounding environment.

The meditation taught at the end of this chapter offers you the genuine possibility of contributing directly to the benefit of all other people. Although the results are neither immediately tangible nor measurable, the practice of the world-healing meditation is an important and positive individual contribution to a safer and more peaceful world. Throw yourself into the world-healing meditation, and, as you become proficient, teach others how to do this meditation.

What can the ordinary person do to reduce the possibility of a nuclear holocaust?

Our capacity to devastate ourselves and our world, through the use of nuclear power, is the clearest available indicator of widespread cultural ignorance that <u>this</u> is <u>that</u>. Our political, military, commercial and industrial systems are organised, directed and run by profoundly unenlightened men and women. We are reliant on political leaders whose mandates are invariably based on the promotion of divisive and factional self-interest.

Our leaders are not to be blamed for this fragmented and dangerous state of affairs. They are washed here and there by the enormous currents of negative karma sweeping across our ignorant and suffering world. Lacking any coherent framework or strategy, they stumble from crisis to crisis.

The intense world-suffering characteristic of late-twentieth century life will cease when the negative karma, accumulated over centuries and coming to fruition in our time, is neutralised. Negative karma on a global scale can only be neutralised, or rendered inactive, by the sustained and committed activity and efforts of enlightened, and relatively enlightened, people. As a result of the progress you have made along the path to enlightenment, you are now able to make a significant contribution to the world-healing process: the process of neutralising negative karma.

There is an activity which you can undertake, on your own initiative, to neutralise the world's accumulated negative karma. You can also teach it to, and engage in this activity with, any number of other people. The minimum requirement to participate successfully in this activity of world-healing is that the participant must have attained the first or psychological stage of enlightenment.

You must be very patient, and have great faith, when undertaking this activity of world healing. It will take the sustained effort of many people in many countries to neutralise the huge amounts of negative karma threatening to devastate our world. It will only happen if you, and all the other people released into or towards enlightenment by fully developed models of reality, proceed with selfless dedication, detachment and commitment.

The causes of the abiding late-twentieth century fear of nuclear holocaust can be healed by the sustained practice of the world-healing meditation taught at the end of this chapter. The practice of this meditation by you is a significant and important contribution to world peace. Undertaken with humility and faith in its effectiveness, it will, in time, bring about a cessation of the profound disharmony expressing itself as the potential for nuclear devastation.

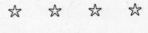

What can the ordinary person do to reduce the possibility of race war?

Observe the manifestations of karmic activity as reported in the news media. Your mind is now responsive to the patterns of karma evident in the world, according to the degree of your spiritual progress. Observe with detachment, not horror, the steadily increasing karmic indicators of widespread race war.

These indicators are to be found in every culture, every nation and every political grouping. Simply watch, listen to and read the news broadcasts. Walk the streets of your own locality with a clear mind, witnessing what does and does not occur, without judgement.

Look beyond the race riots, in your own country or in some other country. Look deeper than the ever more likely race war in South Africa. Witness the ordinary, everyday explicit or implicit racist attitudes which masquerade as objective comment in the media and in ordinary conversation.

Every country fouls the lives of some of its citizens. Every oppressing group looks away, ignoring the way it fouls the lives of others. When an oppressed group protests that it is getting covered in filth, the oppressing group usually accuses it of being covered in filth.

The reality of our late-twentieth century situation is simple and brutal. If the existing negative karma is not neutralised, there will be widespread race war within and between nations. No country will be exempt, because every country has oppressed citizens who are becoming less willing to tolerate the oppression and injustice. No country, no city, no town or village, no street will be exempt.

You have made progress towards becoming a fully conscious component of the one unified reality, through having attained at least the first stage of enlightenment. Do not waste your time pointing out to other people the stupidity and ignorance of their attitudes. From your own experience, you should know not to interfere with other people's fulfilment of their negative karma.

The world's history will unfold as it unfolds, without your interference. Yet you must <u>Act</u> to lessen the possibility of vicious, destructive and futile race wars. You must strive to cleanse yourself and those in your sphere of influence of negative karma.

You must throw yourself with commitment and dedication into the world-healing process. Practise daily the world-healing meditation.

123

Practise it and teach it to others, with unshakeable faith in its healing powers.

☆   ☆   ☆   ☆

What can you do to reduce the profound imbalances between wealth and poverty in our world?

Both individually and as a culture, as we lose sight of the unchanging reality that this is that, so, too, do we desire more and more of this. Enmeshed in the illusion that this is real in itself, we desire love, wealth, sex, fame, power and so on, according to our conditions and our individuality. In an age bereft of transcendentally vibrant models of reality, material success and fulfilment of the senses become the culturally approved goals.

Both individually and collectively, as we begin to regain a vision of the unchanging, all-embracing, transcendent nature of reality, so, too, can we come to accept that our true material needs are modest. Transcending the illusion, recognising and acting on the sound basis that this does not exist in itself but is a dependent product of that, we can learn to accept that what we receive is adequate for our true needs – provided that, as a minimum, we are able to feed ourselves and to have shelter, warmth, education, health, and a life free from unacceptable interference and control. In an age transformed, enlivened and enlightened by relevant and vividly alive models of reality, material success and prosperity tend to become much less important, both collectively and individually.

You will know from your own experience, as a relatively enlightened person, that progress along the spiritual path is neither hindered nor assisted by the absence or presence of money. The key to spiritual progress is freedom from attachment to this. Aware of the true nature of reality, rich or poor in material terms, you now live a life of inner wealth.

Witness now the gross obscenity of Western wealth and Eastern poverty. Witness the West's constant struggle to remain materially wealthy, and witness the East's constant struggle to acquire material prosperity. Observe with compassion the true spiritual poverty of East and West in the late-twentieth century.

This world-wide spiritual poverty can be alleviated through a growth in understanding of the relevance of transcendentally vibrant models of reality in everyday life. A shift in economic priorities can become politically acceptable when the will of the people is directed towards healing this. With the growth of widespread spiritual understanding will come a desire for economic policies capable of alleviating the developing countries' material poverty, and as such policies become vote-winners there will arise politicians who are capable of implementing them.

Your contribution is twofold to this process of cultural maturing in attitudes to material needs. Firstly, live modestly in relation to your material circumstances, and follow your intuition in using what resources you have to spare for the benefit of others. Secondly, commit yourself to practising and teaching the world-healing meditation.

How do you prepare for practice of the world-healing meditation?

This meditation is best practised either in solitude or in peaceful companionship. Choose any meditation posture with which you are both familiar and comfortable. Daily practice for a minimum of fifteen minutes will be best, but this is not essential – every selfless contribution to the general good is of value.

Unlike your everyday Implicate Technology meditations, the world-healing meditation is not a practice which leads to progressively enhanced states of consciousness. Rather, it works on the basis of cleansing and purifying your own psycho-physiological system, and the environment which that is capable of influencing. You are capable of beginning to practise this meditation successfully once you have attained the first stage of enlightenment, and you make progress in its stages according to your level of spiritual development.

The world-healing meditation is based on a simple technique of increasingly focused visualisation, according to your level of consciousness. The purer and clearer the process of visualisation, the greater is the benefit to yourself and others. As you progress in your ordinary meditative practices, so you will be able to experience this meditation at its deeper levels.

Approach the world-healing meditation with a humble sense of giving what you are able to, for the benefit of others. Be warned: practising this meditation with a sense of complacency or smugness about your own virtue and selflessness will ensure that you experience karmic activity

125

structured to teach you true humility. Use your meditative skills to ignore any self-centred, self-oriented thoughts which may arise as you meditate.

If you are ill and seeking to purify your psycho-physiological system through this meditation, then it is best to concentrate your efforts largely for your own benefit. Be clear: all illness is caused by a preponderance of negative karma, associated with your individual mind, your body or your environment. These karmic imbalances can occur in any degree and combination, and can affect the unenlightened, the relatively enlightened and the enlightened person.

If you are ill and practising the world-healing meditation to heal yourself, dedicate your efforts to identifying and understanding the karmic causes underlying your illness. If you are practising this meditation for your own and the general good, dedicate your efforts to identifying and understanding the prevalent patterns of karmic activity in your environment. In either case, once you have identified and understood the nature of the karma shaping your conditions, dedicate your efforts to harmoniously resolving, balancing and healing the imbalances in the prevailing conditions.

☆   ☆   ☆   ☆

How do you practise the world-healing meditation?

The world-healing meditation is a straightforward visualisation exercise. Simply focus your awareness on the image, as undistractedly as you can manage. The instructions for the meditation, and the inner processes which determine your experience during the meditation, vary at each stage according to how far you have progressed in your spiritual development.

Visualise clear, pure, white light. Visualise the light located at the crown, the very top, of your head. The more you are able to focus your attention only on this image of pure clear white light, and the less attention you pay to distracting thoughts, the greater will be the benefits of this meditation.

Accept with unwavering faith that this meditative activity immerses you in mind in its purest of conditioned states. If you are religious by nature, you should understand this white light as the manifestation of God's love. The greater your ability to concentrate on this visualisation, the greater will be your immersion in the healing powers of mind in its natural state.

126

The clear, pure, white light is mind in its simplest conditioned form, transcending all accumulations of positive and negative karmic influences. As you meditate, you realise mind in its original nature, according to your effort and level of consciousness. Bathed in this light, your psycho-physiological system is cleansed of negative karma; bathed in the love of God, you are cleansed of your sins.

Stage 1: Visualise clear, pure, white light located at the crown of your head. Simply be aware of this image located just on the top surface of your head. If you have attained the first stage of enlightenment, you will be able to maintain this degree of concentration effectively and for an adequate period of time.

Stage 2: With each deep, slow in-breath, the body's inherent sexual energy rises to flow into the purifying light. With each deep, slow out-breath, the body's implicate energy flows downwards, cleansing as it moves. You will be able to maintain this degree of concentration effectively, for at least fifteen minutes, if you have successfully practised the yoga of sexual energy taught in chapter 5 of *Beyond the personality: the beginner's guide to enlightenment*.

Stage 3: Focusing one-pointedly on the pure, clear, white light, the mind's surface activity in response to stimuli fades away and the mind becomes absorbed in the experience of focusing one-pointedly. The focus of awareness moves from the mind's activities to the stillness of mind in its natural state. You will be able to perform this meditation successfully if you have attained the second stage of enlightenment.

Stage 4: Focusing the mind one-pointedly on the clear, pure, white light, the mind becomes absorbed in still, serene contemplation. Witnessing this in tranquillity, observe mind pervading and manifesting everywhere, and experience this as that. You will be able to perform this meditation successfully if you have attained the third stage of enlightenment.

According to your ability, heal yourself and heal the world.

☆   ☆   ☆   ☆

☆   ☆   ☆   ☆

Appendix 3: A secular analogue to the ten sefirot

Introduction

This appendix presents a system of modelling reality and of inter-acting with that model through meditation, which is similar to the Kabbalistic system of the ten sefirot[1]. The modelling technique is based on the meditation system contained in this teach-yourself book, and in *Beyond the personality: the beginner's guide to enlightenment*. These two books together provide a unified, coherent and integrated system of medita-tion, which leads the meditator step by step from ordinary awareness, with all its stress and anxiety, to the peace and serenity of enlight-enment.

The model of reality

The model analyses reality in terms of ten fundamental conditions which influence the life of each person. These conditions are the inescapable forces which shape each moment we experience. Just as the ten sefirot express an intuitive understanding of the formative forces shaping everyday experience from a Jewish mystical viewpoint, so, too, does the meditative system taught in these books express an under-standing of the same forces from a perspective rooted in ordinary experience.

The diagrammatic representation of the ten conditions, which shape daily experience, differs from the traditional Kabbalistic ways of representing the ten sefirot. In the secular model of reality, the ten conditions, as discussed in chapter 3 of *Beyond the personality: the beginner's guide to enlightenment*, naturally fall into a pyramid shape in four levels:

---

[1] Hoffman Edward; *The Way of Splendour: Jewish Mysticism and Modern Psychology*; Boulder, Shambhala, 1981, pages 53–54.

		Karma		Level 1

Space	Time	Level 2

Physical	Intellectual	Emotional	Level 3

Moral	Social	Economic	Political	Level 4

Karma, as discussed in detail in chapter 4 of *Beyond the personality*, is the shaping or formative aspect of reality. In religious terms karma represents the will of God, to which we are all subject. Karma is the process whereby reality structures the circumstances of each person's life, to guide each person towards the next step along the path to re-union with God, or enlightenment.

On the mundane level, the conditions of space and time represent where and when events occur. As practice in meditation-enhanced analysis advances, space and time become understood as the constantly fluctuating context within which events unfold. The advanced meditative practices in *Towards effortless activity* teach two points: firstly, that the understanding of events is relative to their context, and secondly, that in the final analysis of the meditatively-enhanced mind, both space and time are illusory products of mind in its unenlightened state.

The conditions represented in levels 3 and 4 are already accessible to ordinary intelligent people. The personal limiting factors shaping the individual's life, in level 3, are a familiar part of many people's thinking about themselves. The wider cultural constraints and pressures, in level 4, are the constant subject of much of our television, radio, cinematic and printed output.

How is the model of reality integrated with meditation?

Diligent practice of the basic meditation, for about one hundred days for a minimum of fifteen minutes a day, as taught in *Beyond the personality*, leads to a state of calm detachment. As this detachment from one's emotional and intellectual limiting factors grows, it becomes possible to analyse the ten conditions with meditation-enhanced skills. That is to say, the mind skilled in meditation is able to focus on the analysis of the ten conditions with such single-mindedness and intensity of concentration, that the mind's inherent powers of intuition rise to the forefront of consciousness.

The development of intuition is a key aim of any meditative system which forms part of a path to unity with God, or enlightenment. It is through the mind's intuitive realisation of the true nature of perceptible reality, that the illusion of individuality, and the subsequent separateness from each other and God, is dispelled. Intuition, or the sixth sense as it is otherwise known, provides direct experience of the integrated, unified and harmonious nature of the world underlying the apparent separateness and disharmony of everyday life.

With the mind poised, calm and centred in the midst of conditions as a result of the practice of meditation, the process of analysing a situation in terms of the ten conditions comes to a spontaneous and unforced conclusion. Following a sustained period of meditative analysis of conditions, understanding of a situation configures in a lightning flash of intuition. The sudden burst of intuitive understanding creates the possibility of harmoniously transforming the situation under analysis through meditation-enhanced action.

How can meditation-enhanced action creatively and harmoniously transform a set of conditions?

Act according to your intuition
Action which stems from a person functioning in the normal ranges of consciousness is determined by that person's range of needs and desires. Action stemming from a person functioning in the expanded ranges of consciousness, which are accessible through sustained practice of meditation, is determined by that person's capacity to recognise and express the promptings of intuition. Intuition, enhanced by structured meditation, is the guide to transpersonal and unselfish action. In religious terms, intuition is the voice of God directing the individual ever onwards on the journey towards unity with God.

Don't interfere
Intuition, made stronger and more accessible by meditation, results in action which does not interfere with the natural and harmonious flow of reality. Self-willed, selfish action interferes with the natural flow of events. In religious terms, acting intuitively without interfering is the way to make oneself receptive to the will of God.

Just let things happen
Reality flows according to its inherent laws; in religious terms, the world moves according to God's will. A person who interferes with self

or others incurs a compensating response from reality through the activity of karma; a sinner is chastised by a loving God. A mind cleansed of ignorance of the unified nature of reality by sustained practice of meditation knows and accepts, with intuitive certainty, that reality always and only unfolds in its own implacable way.

Summary

This secular model of reality provides a way of analysing the forces which shape everyday situations. It incorporates the purposive and unifying aspect of reality in the condition of karma, which is expressed from a religious perspective as God's will. It also allows for the growth of awareness of the transcendent unity underlying the apparent separation of people places and things, through understanding the illusory nature of space and time when explored from transcendental perspectives.

The meditative system taught in this book and *Beyond the personality*, provides an assured and reliable practical framework for the development of intuition. It is through the mind's natural powers of intuitive perception that the absolute transcendental nature of reality, which manifests itself as the material world accessible through the five senses, can be directly experienced. As intuition springs to life through daily practice of the simple meditation, understanding of the particular conditions being analysed crystallises in a flash, like lightning.

Intuition, enhanced by daily practice of meditation, produces action which crystallises the creative and transforming potential of a situation. For an action to be in harmony with the flow of events it must not interfere with self or others. The attitude of enlightened acceptance is to just let things happen.

<u>Act</u>

Act according to your intuition

Don't interfere

Just let things happen

131

Bibliography

The first stage of enlightenment

The Implicate Technology Centre; *Beyond the personality: the beginner's guide to enlightenment*; London, The Implicate Technology Centre, 1987.
Wilhelm, Richard and Jung, C. G.; *The Secret of the Golden Flower*; London, Routledge & Kegan Paul, 1962.

Channeling the body's inherent implicate energy system

Chia, Mantak; *Awaken Healing Energy Through the Tao*; New York, Aurora Press, 1983.
Chia Mantak; *Taoist Secrets of Love: Cultivating Male Sexual Energy*; New York, Aurora Press, 1984

The second, third and fourth stages of enlightenment

Evans-Wentz, W. Y.; *Tibetan Yoga and Secret Doctrines*; Oxford, Oxford University Press, 1967.
Nanamoli, Bhikkhu; *The Life of the Buddha: According to the Pali Canon*; Kandy, Buddhist Publication Society, 1978.
Shearer, Alexander; *Effortless Being: the Yoga Sutras of Patanjali*; London, Wildwood House, 1982.

The experience of enlightenment

Godman, David; *Be As You Are: the Teachings of Sri Ramana Maharshi*; London, Arkana, 1985.
Sri Ramanasramam; *Talks with Sri Ramana Maharshi*; Tiruvannamalai, T. N. Venkataraman, 1984.
Radhakrishnan, S.; *The Bhagavadgita*; London, George Allen and Unwin Ltd, 1970.

The world-healing meditation

Gyatso, Thubten; *Medicine Buddha Sadhana*; London, Wisdom Publications, 1982.

Glossary

Centred in the midst of conditions: the state of mind, attained on realising the **first stage of enlightenment,** which marks the start of the process of learning to understand the true nature of **reality**.

Clear setting face to face with reality: the **fourth and final stage of enlightenment**; re-unification with God.

Conditions: the ten fundamental forces shaping each moment.

Enlightenment: the progressive states of awareness which, stage by stage, sweep aside ignorance of the nature of **reality**. Enlightenment culminates in the realisation that all of **this** is an organic unity, and is **that** alone. The religious mind experiences enlightenment as re-unification with God, who alone is.
    First stage of enlightenment: realised by attaining detachment from emotional and intellectual conditions.
    Second stage of enlightenment: realised through experiencing the mind's inherent stillness and serenity.
    Third stage of enlightenment: realised when the individual mind has been **transcended**, and perceptible reality is intuitively known to be divine, and only divine.
    Fourth stage of enlightenment: realised when the transcendentally awakened mind becomes one with **reality**.

Explicate: referring to aspects of **reality** which can be understood by the five senses.

Implicate: referring to aspects of **reality** which can only be understood by the sixth sense, or intuition.

Implicate technology: 1) The generic name for the underlying structure and practical techniques for expanding awareness, common to all fully developed models of **reality**.
2) A practical technique, the correct use of which enables the individual to understand and harmonise with the **implicate** aspects of **reality**.

Implicate Technology: a Western-originated, fully developed model of **reality**, incorporating meditative techniques which work in a secular, everyday context.

Karma: 1) An inherent, implacable, **implicate** law of **reality**.
2) The process whereby **reality** structures the circumstances of your life, to guide you towards, onto, then along the path towards **enlightenment**.
3) The law whereby your current thoughts and actions determine your future experience.
4) God's will.

Meditation: 1) The practical process of achieving a still mind, or **samadhi**.
2) The self-help technique which enables you to reach **enlightenment**.
3) A practical technique which awakens the sixth sense, or intuition.

Model of reality: a structured, coherent description of **reality**, which uses practical techniques enabling the individual to experience the unity of **reality**.

Natural state: mind, free of the constraints of the ten **conditions**, clear, serene and blissfully self-aware.

One-pointed meditation: a mind which has realised the **second stage of enlightenment** is capable of concentrating on one object for long enough to intuitively discern its underlying nature.

Personality: the complex of views, opinions, ideas, emotions and attitudes comprising ordinary, everyday awareness. This complex is experienced as real to ordinary consciousness, as relatively real once the **first stage of enlightenment** has been attained, and as illusory once the **final stage of enlightenment** has been realised.

Power discipline: 1) A smooth, harmonious action in three steps: Input, Pivot then Act.
2) A meditative methodology to aid in the process of finding a harmonious and unselfish resolution to any difficult situation.

Reality: the total of what can be known and experienced. In religious terms, reality is the manifest form of God who alone is. The true nature of reality can only be understood once the **final stage of enlightenment** has been experienced.

Samadhi: the state of mind, transcending thought, in which consciousness focuses on the divine source of perceptible **reality**.

Sexual energy: 1) The body's spontaneously generated **implicate** power source.
2) The power inherent in the psycho-physiological system which is refined and transformed, consciously or unconsciously, in advanced meditative activity.

This: the conditioned form of **reality**, the manifest form of God.

That: the divine source and the true nature of perceptible **reality**.

Transcendence: the process whereby the mind moves from ordinary, everyday awareness of separation, suffering and individuality to an all-embracing awareness of unity, harmony and serenity.

Undistracted alertness: 1) The essential attribute of the mind capable of holding fast to the divine nature inherent in perceptible **reality**.
2) The state of **samadhi**.

Unconditioned state: mind in its original state, transcending and embracing all thought and all experience – serene, free and blissfully self-aware.

Visions: an autonomous subjective process, produced as a by-product of advanced meditative practices.

Yoga: the practical techniques for developing awareness and understanding of the **implicate** nature of **reality**.

Synopsis of Contents

TEACH YOURSELF ENLIGHTENMENT!

Stop wondering – start understanding

* self-help guide to enlightenment
* simple technique
* practise for 15 minutes daily
* no teacher needed
* no membership or fees
* not a religion, no-one will call

Send for your copy today using the form below.

To: Dept A99, BCM ACT, London WC1N 3XX

From: (BLOCK CAPITALS PLEASE)

NAME _____

ADDRESS _____

_____

_____ POSTCODE_____

Please send me:

_____ copies at £4.95 each   Total £_____

of *Beyond the personality: the beginner's guide to enlightenment*

_____ copies at £4.95 each   Total £_____

of *Towards effortless activity: the advanced guide to enlightenment*

Remittance enclosed   £_____

Please make cheques payable to: The Implicate Technology Centre
Prices include packaging and postage
Please allow up to 21 days for delivery

TEACH YOURSELF ENLIGHTENMENT!

Stop wondering – start understanding

* self-help guide to enlightenment
* simple technique
* practise for 15 minutes daily
* no teacher needed
* no membership or fees
* not a religion, no-one will call

Send for your copy today using the form below.

_____

To: Dept A99, BCM ACT, London WC1N 3XX

From: (BLOCK CAPITALS PLEASE)

NAME _____

ADDRESS _____

_____

_____ POSTCODE_____

Please send me:

_____ copies at £4.95 each   Total £_____

of *Beyond the personality: the beginner's guide to enlightenment*

_____ copies at £4.95 each   Total £_____

of *Towards effortless activity: the advanced guide to enlightenment*

Remittance enclosed   £_____

Please make cheques payable to: The Implicate Technology Centre
Prices include packaging and postage
Please allow up to 21 days for delivery